Tending Your Garden

Tending Your Garden

Wisdom for Keepers at Home

Denise Sproul

TOLLE LEGE PRESS
WHITEHALL, WEST VIRGINIA

Tending Your Garden:
Wisdom for Keepers at Home

Copyright © 2008 Denise Sproul
Published by **Tolle Lege Press**
P.O. Box 5059
White Hall, WV 26555

Cover by Joseph Darnell
Interior layout by Luis Lovelace

Printed in the United States of America

ISBN13: 978-1-60702-149-0

In Dedication

To Joe and Betty Lou Rocklein,
RC and Vesta Sproul:
with thankfulness for your love and guidance.

To my husband, RC, Jr:
I am blessed to be your helpmeet.
You make our garden a beautiful, joyful place.
The Lord smiled on me the day
He joined us together!

Contents

FOREWORD   9

ONE: Tending Your Garden   11

TWO: Support and Submit   39

THREE: Sanctification in
          Child Training   53

FOUR: Diligence   83

FIVE: Protection and Peace   101

SIX: The Fruit of the Spirit   121

Foreword

by Carol DeMar

Gardening has long been one of my life's pleasures. I remember our very first garden. Its size exceeded my plans to maintain it! I thought how splendid it would be for the children and me to plant seeds, watch tiny shoots pop up from the ground and slowly grow into mature plants, producing vegetables and fruit that we would enjoy at our table. There was nothing slow about it! We had a very hot summer with much rainfall. My sons' small hands couldn't begin to keep up with the weeding. I was giving away much more food than we could eat. If I didn't pick the okra each day, it would get too big and lose its flavor. I still remember that first garden most fondly, but future gardens were definitely downsized!

Digging in the dirt has provided many lessons over the years for our family, so when I began reading Denise Sproul's book, I was taken in immediately because of the gardening theme that runs throughout the subject of being a godly wife. The reader is in for a delightful journey as Denise weaves a gentle path toward the true role of wife and mother, using examples of gardening to reinforce her points.

I had the pleasure of having dinner on board ship in the Hawaiian Islands with an intimate group of people which included R.C. Sproul, Sr., his wife Vesta and their daughter

Sherry and her husband. We ladies sat at one end of the table while the men sat at the other. While they spoke of deep theological issues, we women enjoyed speaking on many various subjects. Actually, I think our end of the conversation was much more interesting! At one point, Vesta and Sherry asked me if I had ever met Denise. I had met R.C., Jr., her husband, but not Denise. When the highest praise for someone comes from in-laws, that is praise indeed! I finally met Denise, and though our time together was short, I was not disappointed. She is a lovely woman, and her inner beauty comes forth in this book. Her gentleness and warmth are genuine. I can just imagine her with her husband and children, who are blessed to be sure. Denise does not preach, nor does she simply give you an opinion; she declares the truth that comes from God's Word and delivers it in a most graceful manner.

In today's mixed up world, *Tending Your Garden* provides women a compass to guide them in their quest to be godly wives. Wives who strive to be godly are much absent, even in Christian circles. Women have been sucked in by the world's standards and too often attempt to be the kind of overbearing women portrayed in the media. Woe to us, if we miss out on the blessed opportunity that God offers to the woman who seeks His righteousness. Matthew 6:33 tells us "But seek first His kingdom and His righteousness and all these things shall be added to you." What things? All that we need and more, He will provide. Read and heed the words of *Tending Your Garden*. Your life, and that of your family, will be blessed as you seek to be the wife and mother God has called you to be.

CHAPTER ONE

Tending Your Garden

The home is the center of our garden as Christian women. As old-fashioned as it may sound, it's actually a biblical idea: a woman's realm is her husband, her children and her home. While many of us delight in this sphere to which God has called us, homemaking is no simple task. It is not for the simple-minded or the faint of heart. In this first chapter, we will consider various domains and circumstances over which the godly woman is to preside.

Spinderella

Ladies, think back to the last form you had to fill out where there was a space for you to list your occupation. What did you write? The idea of "spin" refers to how we have our thoughts skewed by the careful wording of our enemies and how we sometimes make the same mistakes. "Spin" causes even us as Christian women to devalue calling.

We all laugh when someone "jokingly" asks, "Do you work, or do you stay at home?" We sometimes shrug it off, thinking it's natural for someone to wonder what our work is, and we overlook the fact that they might actually think it's weird not to have a "real job." The fact that many of us have to uncomfortably assert ourselves by saying, "Yes, I work, and yes, I stay at home," shows that many people think that each is mutually exclusive of the other. We should never speak in this way ("work" or "home"—i.e. lazy couch potato) and we should always kindly correct it. If a man asks you this question, you might politely counter with, "Do you work, or do you raise children?"

Make sure you know that God has called you to work (see Genesis 2). Do not look at your work as something you have to hurry up and do to get to the fun stuff, with an attitude of "working for the weekend." I remember when I was single and teaching school having even my attitude about washing dishes change when I heard Elisabeth Elliot speak of "doing all to the glory of God." Working heartily as unto the Lord applies to whatever tasks He gives us to do each day, no matter how mundane they may seem. Seek to delight in your work and recognize it as work, don't try to rename it as play. Work hard and delight in the toil God has given you.

This spin which devalues women's work in the home actually precedes the modern feminist movement. Women used to be described as "housewives," as if they were married to their houses. This may be because so many women had only their houses to take care of and not so much their children, with the children gone a large part of each day at school and often gone in the summer at camp. Your job is not to be a wife to a house, but a wife to your husband and a mother to your children, if God has so blessed you.

The word "homemaker" is better than "housewife" because it is a much better representation of what you do and encompasses much more the heart of what your work is about.

Other options include "keeper at home" (you are keeping the home running, with all the myriad jobs and delights that involves), or "garden tender", or for those with small children, "tender garden tender" (I can't take the credit or blame for that last one. R.C. gave it to me!) No one will take our role seriously unless we take it seriously ourselves. This includes the necessity of working hard and also refusing to be apologetic about doing our God-given task, as if we were doing work of second-rate importance and are just too lazy to have outside work. If you are ever tempted to believe that nonsense about yourself or know someone else who thinks that about you, perhaps you should invite them to come over and spend, oh, maybe about your typical 16-hour work day. Even if they just sit and watch you, they'll probably go home exhausted!

I don't really mean that you should have someone over like that to prove the validity of your work. You are accountable to your husband and to the Lord. We need to remember to tend our gardens. Do not neglect your calling by going on a crusade to defend your calling. Don't form some sort of NAAGT—the National Association for the Advancement of Garden Tenders. You are not a victim; if your focus is on your garden, you won't care whether people think you're napping in the bean patch when you are actually hoeing a tough row. Neither should you fuss unduly at people in your own life who mistakenly use this "work or homebody" distinction. Just make sure you and your children do not believe it.

As an aid to not believing the world's spin, it also helps to avoid taking in the folly of the world. Steer clear of the Oprahs and the "ladies" magazines that aren't written by or for real ladies. Most magazines on a typical newsstand do not promote the godly values of being Titus 2 women. What they do is teach you to long for a life to which you weren't called, to make you feel like you are missing out. Besides, if you are working like you should, you won't have time for that kind of nonsense (and don't let that send you on a pity party—that is as it should be!) When you are working hard and teaching your children to do the same, and they complain about the difficulty of their work after they know how to do it, you can not only teach them a lesson about "doing all things without grumbling or complaining." Remind them (and yourself, silently) that yes, much of our work is hard and that God made it that way. Resist the urge to entice them by saying, "Oh no, this is easy!" You will be inadvertently teaching them to avoid things that are in fact hard.

So back to my original question: What do you put in that little box on the form that asks what you do—short of writing an essay? If you don't already, think about it next time and don't write your answer angrily, defensively or apologetically. Try to choose a word or two that describes the joyous, glorious work you have been granted the privilege of doing. Whether others know it or not, as homemakers and as handmaidens of the Lord, no "working woman" should be able to outwork us, for we work for our greater Husband, Jesus our King.

War of the Weeds

Most of us, I pray, are not such feminists that we would say women should go out on the battlefield, fighting for their country. So how do we women wage war? Are we excluded from everything to do with warfare? When God talks about "the weapons of our warfare" or "the gates of Hell not prevailing against us," does He put a qualifier in those verses to let us know He is only addressing the men?

Femininity ought not to be equated with passivity or weakness. That we do not take up arms doesn't mean our arms are weak. Our idea of godly womanhood should not be confused with the Victorian idea of lounging women who frequently suffer from "the vapors." That feminists try to make men of women, however, does not mean that we should view women as *children*; failing to give them credit for and responsibility to understand things, taking care of themselves and their families.

As women we are on the front line of the real war, because we are about the business of training the next generation of soldiers—teaching our children that, "I'm in the Lord's army. Yes sir!" Such training is itself an act of war—a declaration to the world and to the powers of darkness that we will not sit back and let someone else's sinful agenda reign, letting our children be tossed to and fro by every wind of doctrine that seeks to lead them astray.

As with the endless clothes that need to be washed, this battle never has a cease fire. We actually don't ever truly have a furlough either, since even while we may be on vacation with our families the training does not stop. You don't have your child sass you while you're enjoying a day at the beach and say, "Oh well, that's O.K. We're on vacation. Let's just enjoy our time. I don't want the day to end on a sour note."

As we are about the business of tending our gardens, we must remain ever vigilant about beating back the weeds. These weeds, of course, begin in our own hearts, in the form of habits of thinking and doing. "As a man thinks in his heart, so is he"

(Proverbs 23:7). We must be diligent in thinking biblically, which means we must regularly be reading Scripture. You know the old saying, "Garbage in, garbage out." You can't be faithfully instructing your children in righteousness if you are constantly trying to draw from a dry well.

Many of the weeds in our hearts and lives are second and third generation weeds that are very difficult to eradicate. If we pull them out carefully and firmly, making sure that we get those tenacious, strong roots, we do our children and grandchildren a great service. Imagine if we just left them or only pulled off the ugly top part, neglecting the roots. Our grandchildren would have a very difficult task, trying to uproot five or six generations worth of bad habits! If we suffer from bitterness or ingratitude or insecurity, we teach those things to our children by example, and it continues to get passed down the line. Then it is no longer just a temptation to be worked against, but a habit and lifestyle to be changed.

While we are pulling out the weeds in our own lives, seeking to diligently serve the Lord Christ, we need to simultaneously be turning to the weeds that grow in the hearts of our children. This requires keeping an eye on them, carefully observing their fruit and soil conditions. Also, are any of your plants crowding the others? I'm not suggesting separate bedrooms for everyone; I'm suggesting keeping close tabs on how they treat their siblings and other family members. All of this observation needs to then lead to action—fertilizing with the Word and encouragement to stimulate godly growth. This fertilizing helps make your plants strong so that the weeds are crowded out and you are instilling good habits in your children. It also involves the right exercise of discipline, including the weed whacker!

We have all seen overgrown gardens—where there may well be lovely flowers, but they cannot be seen for all the weeds. I think that is one of my most discouraging times— when I see my outside ("real") garden and know how pretty it could look if I had more time. But then I remind myself that I have inside weeding to do also, and God requires me to make time for that. If our toddler is frequently fussing loudly when Shannon has a toy she suddenly decides she wants, I have some weeding to do in the form of instruction and firm "no's." I also need to make sure my other children are not encouraging weed growth in her (albeit well-meaning) by giving her another similar toy right away or giving Shannon something else so that the toddler can have the coveted toy. You can't have your children sowing weed seed.

Sometimes others can't see the flowers in our gardens for the weeds. It can be very helpful to ask the master gardeners in your life (not the professionals, but your godly friends whose flowers can frequently be seen) for insight and counsel. They may be able to identify weeds you are unaware of and can help get you started on an eradication program. This is also a good opportunity for you to praise and encourage them for the good cultivating they have done. Most of us find it easy to find fault and not so easy to remember to speak sincere compliments.

To fight with vigor, we must remember what is at stake. This is not a petty war over such things as who will govern the world in the here and now, but over who will rule in eternity. This will have far more impact than mere weapons that can kill the body but will never touch the soul. If we love our little flowers, we will want them to live forever, to beautify the Master's garden into eternity and to enjoy the sunlight of His loving gaze. So press on; nothing matters more.

Dwelling Among Them

While we generally don't talk about such things, it is good and proper that the Incarnation should comfort us. We often forget that we are God's children, and put on a stiff upper lip (which matches the rest of us—stiff). But God was and is here among us; for those in Christ, He is here not in judgment. He is here with us for an important reason—because He loves us.

We are not only God's children, but to quote the psychologist Dr. Laura, we are also our children's parents. This means that in many ways, we are God in the flesh to them (just as, for us wives, our husbands are like Jesus to us). Our word, according to God's word, and like God's word, is law. We, like God, provide protection for our children. We provide, through God's grace, our children's daily bread. We are, again through God's grace, their creators. Just as the husband and wife are pictures of Jesus and the church, so the parent/child relationship is a picture of the Creator and creature. There are definitely limitations to this analogy, but that doesn't undo the principle and practice we can derive from looking at it somewhat loosely.

Now, assuming we can go ahead with this analogy of representing God in the flesh to our children, here is where it takes us: if we would be God in the flesh to our children, we must tabernacle among them. We are against the egalitarianism of this age that tries to make us our children's buddies. We have made a case against segregating families at church. In like manner, we can't allow our anti-egalitarianism to cause us to segregate our homes. To put it more plainly, we need to tabernacle among our children, to spend time with them. And we need to do so with joy, because we love them. If it were legitimate for us to try to picture what God looks like or to imagine a picture of Jesus, can you see Him giving you a hug, yet holding you stiffly at arm's length, with a grimace on His face as if you smelled bad?

Are we really spending time with our children? I was surprised a few years ago to hear that my husband believed the quality versus quantity time theory was a bunch of hogwash. I came to understand why he thought this way. Certainly it is better to play a game with your children than it is to take them with you to the post office, but that doesn't mean we shouldn't take them or that there is nothing good that comes out of running such an errand together. You might actually talk more and about more important things while driving around together than you would while playing a game of Uno. They might learn some practical things as well, while observing how you conduct business. Math lessons, time budgeting, and courteous behavior, even toward workers who are less than helpful, are several lessons they might learn just from being along for the ride with you.

We must not wait until it is "convenient" to spend time with our children. If we did, who of us ever would? When was it convenient for God to dwell among us? He did it, despite setting aside His glory. Certainly we can set aside what we perceive as our convenience in order to joyfully fulfill our obligations toward our children.

So what about practical advice? Daily activities and errands that all of us are required to do are fine times to spend with your precious offspring. I recall reading in Rick Boyer's humorous book, *Yes, They're All Ours* about how he and his wife had various alone time with their fifteen (at that time) children merely by including them in their mundane errands. Often those mundane times became much more profitable and enjoyable because of special time to talk with one or a few of the children. If you can't take them all, take a few with you (and sometimes this works out well to really get them talking). Campbell is our young man who will always say "yes" when asked if he'd like to go get groceries with Dad or do some shopping with Mom. If I ever go without him, he invariably will say to me sometime that day, "I feel like I haven't seen you much lately, Mom." He and Delaney and Darby know the routine for buying chicken feed at the farmer's co-op and the checkout girls at the grocery store always ask about smiley Shannon and Erin Claire if they are not with us. Baking bread and folding laundry are also good times to visit and instruct. It's actually the family that *works* together that stays together.

As fun as this errand running can be, it's still important to find some special time that is more focused and not so distracted with getting things done. We are in the habit of having family worship in the evenings. This is a time of worship for our whole family, reading God's word, praying, and singing together. Several years ago we also started doing individual Bible studies, Darby and Delaney with me and Campbell with Dad. How sweet and effective those times are, not just for the children's edification and sanctification, but for ours as well!

We have also instituted a family night on Wednesday nights. After the little girls are down (and lest you worry that they are left out, they have other individual time with us and will also be included when they get a bit bigger), RC, Campbell, and sometimes Delaney play a game, or do a woodworking project together. Darby and I work on her scrapbook together, try the laniard kit Aunt Sherrie gave her last Christmas, or even work on sewing buttons on the dress it took me a year-and-a-half to finish for her! I know that we'll have to get more creative when Erin Claire, Maili, and Reilly are ready for these evenings, but that doesn't mean it will be impossible. We pray we will do this because we love them and delight in them, not because it's a chore. We would all do well to remember that it is an honor and a wonderful responsibility to reflect the character of God to our children, to remember that He loves His children, and to delight to love ours.

A Well-Oiled Machine?

I am thankful for technology, but am sometimes still confounded by it. Ask any friends of mine who have to wait almost an eternity for an e-mail from me—or ask my husband and son who regularly help me with the most basic computer skills! How do we utilize technology—and therefore, systems—in the home without allowing ourselves to become machine-like? How do we keep the heart of our homes a living, beating, feeling entity rather than a cold machine that's like an automaton? Technology has invaded our homes, just as it has touched every aspect of our world. Sometimes this is a blessing; other times it can be a curse. I am thrilled not to have to rub my family's clothing against a rock in a cold stream somewhere. On the other hand, I'm less than excited about the mountains of clothing we possess that I have to wash and press (though I have gotten smart about that and now have very few items that need to be ironed). The very machine that makes the clothes easier to wash has also seemed to multiply the clothes.

We sometimes allow technology to affect how we view our families; we come to think of our loved ones as a single economic unit (which they are) but look at each family member as a spoke in the wheel, each with an important job to do. While each person in our family does have an important role and function, he is much more than just that. Going to the opposite extreme of this technological view of the family is likewise unhealthy—the romantic reaction of thinking that whatever is "natural" is best. It should occur to us that whatever is natural, since the Fall, includes sin. It is natural for our children to belch, but unless they've just eaten a meal in China, we want to teach them to control certain natural impulses.

We don't desire to just "let things happen naturally," "kick back and relax," "just do whatever floats your boat"—I could go on with the aphorisms, but I'm sure "you get my drift." We want to bring order, intentionality and deliberateness to our family lives. All of us adults—whether or not we will consciously recognize it—want structure and predictability, just as our children do. Part of me is pleased when my husband comments that I run our home like a well-oiled machine; however, I don't want to take this too far. It is a hard thing to find balance though, because if I am tending capably to things like meals, laundry, homeschooling, and cleaning, those things are very outwardly measurable. One can easily look at a clean house with clean children sitting down to a delicious meal and think: "Wow. She's doing everything right." What cannot always be seen are attitudes, lack of time reading to or talking with the children, or an in-tune, how-can-I-help-you-today demeanor towards our husbands. For those of us who may struggle with more of a Martha (as opposed to a Mary, choosing the better portion) outlook, we have to constantly be thinking, "What is my focus? Is it what God wants it to be?"

Children are not machines. Yes, they need order, structure, and of course, discipline, but they cannot be crammed in to fit on an assembly line. Whatever our systems are, they require flexibility. It is good to have a plan for when certain household tasks will be done (lest they remain perpetually undone) but it is not good to allow that plan to lead to hyper-scheduling and insensitivity. If I plan to dust right after breakfast, I don't tell Reilly to wait for me to hold him when he's split his lip. If playtime at the park is planned for Saturday morning, I don't drag my children out in the rain or try to bring the swingset inside. Now, I know as you ponder the two solutions to these dilemmas, you might be thinking, "Oh, I would never do that! How ridiculous!" But how many of us would have a bad attitude about the disruptions to our plans? Do we look at these disruptions as divine intervention—as opportunities for obedience, things that are also part of God's plan for our lives for that day—or do we think as we're holding our crying child, "Now how do I rearrange the rest of the day so that my house is clean?"

Resist the urge to think that all structure and planning is bad. Being like Jesus' friend Mary does not mean sitting back and letting life happen to you. We are called to live life simply, separately and deliberately. God does exhort us to do things "decently and in order." We are not to be constantly flying by the seat of our pants and praying that when we land, we're all in one piece. "You shall not tempt the Lord your God"

(Luke 4:12). Being loving and sensitive is not to be equated with being wishy-washy and undisciplined. As in many cases, balance is the key. If our focus and structure is too narrow, we scrunch our loved ones in to fit our agendas. If it is too broad, our families turn to jelly—no one seems to know which way is up. We must also always keep our eyes on the prize: our goal is to raise godly seed, not well-ordered heathen. We must teach our children to be orderly and disciplined, but must also teach them with our words and with our actions what Christ's love is like. If I grudgingly hold my hurt child, I'm teaching him that love is rude. If I have a fit when we can't go to the park, I'm teaching them that love is impatient. We want to see our godly seed flourish into godly men and women. Be like Christ to your children, never fail to take them into your arms and bless them. Never fail to suffer the children to come unto you.

Mary Versus Martha

It is clear from Scripture that we are to be hospitable in our homes and that we are to welcome especially brothers and sisters in Christ into our midst on a regular basis. This is for the purpose of edifying and serving one another, showing the love of our Lord. We are all familiar with the Mary and Martha story where Martha gets bent out of shape during Jesus' visit because she perceived that Mary was not helping enough with meal preparation. We also know Jesus' response to Martha's accusation: He told her that Mary had chosen the better portion by sitting down and listening to His teaching. We know that we are supposed to be like Mary, but still struggle with being Martha. Our calling is to choose the necessary thing, yet we still feel the pull of wanting the finer things. We get obsessed (read: idolatrous) about wanting our homes, our meals, our yards to be beautiful. While we know that Lazarus is the one who was raised from the dead, it sometimes seems as if Martha is the one still with us. We see her everywhere— from the TV to the newsstand to K-Mart. She has apparently remarried, for now she goes by the name of Martha Stewart. While I appreciate her pretty sheets, reasonably priced flower bulbs and her garden rakes, I do not appreciate how my sinful nature can get overly interested in acquiring those things and spending too much time putting them to use.

Both the world and the church are awash in hints on beautifying our lives (there's Martha and then there's Emilie Barnes—whose books I have greatly enjoyed). This is fine and good as long as we don't take it too far. What follows is not an argument for serving hot dogs to our guests on paper plates while we sit in our living room on plastic lawn furniture. It is, however, a call to not miss out on the better, a call not to miss the point in our Christian hospitality.

Some balk at the thought of having others in their homes; they see it as putting on a show and feel ill-equipped. There are two reasons we are tempted to put on a show when we have company. First, we think this is what our guests want. But think about it. When was the last time you left a friend's home all giddy because their flower arrangement looked so nice? What each of us truly enjoys is time spent with our friends and family, in our home or theirs. It's not about wowing or being wowed by culinary expertise. And meeting with friends in a home, even if they are new friends whose approval you desire, is not supposed to be a trip to a museum. The second reason we're tempted to put on a show is so that others will think, "Wow, she really went to a lot of trouble for us." Our desire should be for others to think, "Wow, I really enjoyed talking with her; what a blessing that was."

There are two reasons we must not make these two mistakes associated with seeing hospitality as show time. First, we are to be like Jesus to our guests. That means we give freely of our time, not just our substance. We're more concerned with building one another up in love and spurring one another on to good deeds than we are with spending the whole visit sweating in the kitchen. Second, our Christian guests are to be Jesus to us. They are in union with Christ. Doesn't it then make sense that we would want to be with them rather than carving vegetables for a centerpiece? This means that when we are with these image-bearers of Christ, we need to be completely "there" and not distracted and stressed because the souffle has fallen.

So how do we keep a balance; serving edible food but not a seven course meal? Make sure your guests are comfortable and feel at home, not like they're at a highbrow restaurant. Think of yourself in terms of a waiter, not a cook. You want to serve your guests, freely giving them your attention. Worry more about the cat jumping up on them than about having heart-shaped ice cubes for their drinks. Worry about whether they can rest and relax in your home rather than whether they feel they've had an adventure at your big shindig. Display your concern for their needs, not your need for display. Remember that we show hospitality to others for their sake, not our own. If you feel you need to radically change your home for guests, one legitimate goal would be to work on making your home normally peaceful and orderly.

A few brief words about the flipside of this—being a gracious guest. First, if your host has requested an R.S.V.P., the least you can do is call and respond. I am frequently appalled at the lack of this courtesy, even among Christians. If a bad memory is the culprit for this oversight, put the invitation or a note to yourself in a conspicuous place, so that after you have checked it with your husband, you can answer your host. Another important part of being a kind guest is teaching your children what this means. First, we teach them to be gracious and thankful for the food that they are served—there is no room for complaints. Secondly, we teach them that they may not help themselves to all rooms and toys—only the ones that their host (including the under 10 set) offers them. At the end of the visit, they help put away all the goodies and leave things, as much as possible, the way they found them. This means if the parents have a departure time in mind, they need to prompt the children beforehand to get busy (for some young ones and those new at picking up after themselves, this may also need to be supervised). You want your children to be welcome guests, not ones that require an hour-long cleanup by the host family. Hospitality can and should be a delightful, relaxing joy to all—both hosts and guests.

Ladies In Waiting?

Mothers and daughters today are under assault. They are told by the world that their future lies in getting a job and "making a difference." There are battles out there, social ills that need to be remedied, and we all need to do our part. They are often told a similar tale in the church and given a similar charge: the exercise of dominion, the building of the kingdom is found in getting power jobs (well, they don't often use the phrase "building the kingdom" when giving this advice). It doesn't seem to make a bit of difference if you're a man or a woman—the advice is the same. It is a good and proper thing that we should defend and delight in the calling to be a wife and mother. This is fighting wisely, and it is most definitely biblical. But there is a danger in this approach as well. We have often been, I'm afraid, teaching our daughters that life begins when they marry. Too often, for instance, our attempt at avoiding the emotional train wreck of dating leads to the emotional train wreck of courtship. That is, we allow or even encourage our daughters to get all giddy-eyed and light-headed because they're in the safety of courtship and not spending time alone with a young man out on dates. They then get to jump from having no ties to being engaged, and isn't that exciting and romantic? This, by the way, is not meant to be a denunciation of the whole idea of courtship. There is a proper and healthy way to do it. It does mean, however, that we need to understand that life doesn't begin for us, or our daughters, when they marry. Our daughters were not made to be Ladies in Waiting, but Ladies at Work.

Our daughters need to be taught that they are *now* working to make manifest the reign of Christ, that they are *now* exercising dominion, that they are *now* under authority. This is the same for all believers, no matter what their ages, social standing, marital status or gifts. And what a blessing God has given in that there is a confluence of their work *now* and their work *then*. That is, they are actually at work as they are training to be wives and mothers. And they also learn the virtue of hard work. If they are being trained properly and are doing their work with all diligence, they know that it's rigorous work now and then. It won't come as a surprise to them later that they need to be prayerful, diligent, good planners, able to multi-task, and keep the best interests of their loved ones at the forefront of their minds. But their comfort should not be that they are in training (which will make them all the more impatient for "someday"—sigh), but that they are building the kingdom. They are not just storing up recipes in their recipe boxes to someday prepare for their princes, they are helping their own mother with the meal planning and cooking and bringing a meal to a sick family at church. That's building the kingdom now and not succumbing to the sin of thinking, "Someday when I have someone special to call my own, then my life will begin."

Let me say that marrying my prince at 26, a month shy of 27, I can fully understand a girl's temptation to despair and think she is just waiting for the day when God will answer her prayers and bring her a man. I know it is not easy to wait when you have not yet been given the desire of your heart. Nonetheless, that does not mean we are free to give in to that despondency and think there's nothing we can do about it. There's lots we can do: pray, read what God's Word says about what we should be doing now, and then set about doing it.

Practically speaking, as our daughters get older, they should take on more and more responsibility and be more and more productive. As mothers, we should, under our husbands' guidance and authority, be purposefully planning and training for this increasing responsibility and productivity. Your eleven year old is not just going to wake up one morning knowing how to change the baby and feed him his breakfast. Your fourteen year old is not going to plan a week's worth of suppers and figure out the groceries needed without you putting some effort into teaching her how to do that. And your sixteen year old is not going to diligently seek to be aware of prayer requests of those in the church and other loved ones and be faithfully praying for them if you haven't modeled and taught her how to do that. We all have areas where we need to be more diligent with our children. The challenge is not getting slack and just coasting, but prayerfully considering what God would have you working on with each child.

We have several young ladies in our own community who have been an enormous help to families such as ours. They are regularly involved in helping numerous families with various things—from cooking and cleaning to math tutoring and knitting instruction. They are busy with their own families and others,' lending a hand and making manifest God's kingdom *now* by making 10 peanut butter sandwiches at a time on homemade bread or by taking a special needs child for a walk and showing her the beauty of God's creation right outside her door. They are helping with newly adopted triplets' nighttime feedings and cooking supper and doing play-doh with a three-year-old so that a new mother can take a much-needed rest. This is being about the business of kingdom building *now* which is also preparing them for what their own future will hopefully hold. We pray that these godly, young, kingdom-building ladies will be blessed with godly husbands. But we also pray that they will see their labors *now* as bearing great fruit. We pray in thanksgiving that our own daughters are seeing their godly examples. And we pray that our daughters will do the same as they grow older. We want them to be eager to marry, but to rejoice in their current calling and to labor at it with all diligence.

Knick Knack Nation

I am alternately sad and pleased that they know me by name at the local Junior League Bazaar. They do not know my name because I am a member of the Junior League, I'm not. They know my name because at this store—which is a permanent garage sale, open 5 days a week—I regularly bring things to sell. It's the sort of place that is on a donation or consignment basis. Again, I have been alternately sad and pleased at the amount of money I have earned by consigning things with them. They know RC as well. They have rules about how many items you can consign with them each month. If you have items over that limit, you are allowed to send someone else from your family, who will have his own account there. I guess I should be relieved that I haven't had to open accounts in my children's names. Understand also that I live in a bad location—quite far out in the country—to get much yard sale traffic. So this is one of the few ways I can sell gently used items.

I don't think I ever realized how much junk I had—or to put it more nicely, things I didn't truly need—until I started trying to get rid of some. I didn't realize the magnitude of my problem until I had items to take to the store month after month. And I have been at it for two years! I guess I should have realized the scope of the problem when RC started teasing me about my penchant for purchasing plastic boxes for sorting my junk. And now I've actually taken some of those plastic organizers to sell at the store! Besides RC teasing me about all the plastic, he also gives me a hard time about all the books I've bought that tell how to de-clutter one's home. All I need now is a plastic box in which to keep the books.

It is one of the devil's games to distort the good into something evil. From the beginning in the Garden, women have been more focused on keeping the garden lovely and less on turning jungle into garden. That is, while husbands and wives share duties inherent in the dominion mandate, men look outward, bringing things under subjection. Women look inward and tend and keep the garden. As keepers of our homes, we rightly aspire to make them veritable gardens. They are to be places of beauty and delight and not mere utility. Part of the insanity of the Fall is that we confuse collecting things with beautifying our homes.

What drives this may be less the devil and more Mrs. HGTV. That is, we move from making our homes places of beauty that will be comfortable for our families and friends to making them showplaces for our skills. We go from wanting to make our visitors comfortable when they visit to wanting them to admire our homemaking abilities. For many women it's not about stirring up covetousness, it is a desire for approval and admiration. We go from serving God to serving man, whether it is in trying to keep up with the Joneses or trying to keep up with decorating ideas from our favorite magazine.

It doesn't matter where we are on the economic ladder either. Some collect Hummels while others collect Faberge eggs. While the price tags are different, the spirit is the same. If my focus is on things to the point that I am constantly cleaning out, organizing, regrouping and selling, then something is amiss. It could be simply not getting rid of old things when I bring in the new. Whether it is a case of thinking I might need the old item someday or simply having so much that I don't realize I still have the item, priorities are out of order. I am either putting my security in the things instead of the Lord or devoting too much of my time to making things look nice.

The beauty we seek to build in our homes, however, ought to be informed and suffused by 1 Peter 3:4. The same gentle and quiet spirit that pleases the Lord in our persons—that He finds beautiful—should be what we seek to show forth in our homes. Are our homes a place of peace and quietness (as a general rule)? Are we gentle and kind to one another? Have we kept our focus right so that we're not stressed about having to de-clutter? You know that question—do you run your house or does your house run you? The more we have, the more we need to maintain, fix, and clean. When we really de-clutter, when our homes have a gentle and quiet spirit, we women tend to have a more gentle and quiet spirit. When we have less junk to care for, we are more carefree. Not irresponsible but better able to focus on and attend to things and people that really matter. Our husbands and children (or for you single ladies, your families and friends) are the ones for whom our labors will last. Wouldn't it be wiser to get rid of the wood, hay, and stubble now instead of waiting for it to burn up? Do I want to tell the God of the Universe at the last day that I just had to get those petunias planted or that I saw the greater need and made a healthy supper for my family? There's nothing inherently wrong with petunias; I just need to be sure if I am planting them that I have chosen the better portion. I can't say to the Lord that I would have listened to and advised my husband when he asked but I just had to get those curtains sewn. Or I had to peruse seven catalogs to see which curtains I wanted to purchase and then have a yard sale with all my old junk to be able to afford them. Choosing the better portion and tending our gardens means consciously choosing and seeking beauty and fruitfulness, rather than affirmation from others and clutter.

The Parable of the Talents

When it comes to parenting, in some sense, if we aren't afraid, we aren't doing it right. Of course we haven't been given a spirit of fear. Of course we must also be bold and strong, for the Lord our God is with us wherever we go. Which, come to think about it, is a good reason to fear. The saying that she who rocks the cradle rules the world isn't just about a happy rush of power. It is instead a sobering, heavy burden of responsibility.

Jesus' parable of the talents has a happy coincidence in its name. "Talents" in that day, as is evident from the story, was a word used for money. The principle in the parable, however, can be applied far more broadly. The word does apply to our talents, whatever they may be. But it also applies to our calling, giving us a deeper sense of urgency in the task the Lord has given us. The Master hasn't merely put money into our hands that needs to be invested prudently. He has instead placed in our arms children that will last forever. And we will surely give an account to the Master, for we are simply stewards of His good gifts. It should concern us if we regularly spend more time and attention considering our monetary talents and what we should do with them or how we can increase them than we do with the most precious ones our Lord has given us. We all get distracted at times. But that should not be our regular pattern. If I repeatedly push Maili and Erin Claire aside while I'm painting a room or if I don't discipline when I should because I'm planting and working in the garden, I'm sinning and need to repent. I may be investing, but I'm investing in all the wrong places.

We pray we would never presume to judge our own holiness on a sliding scale. God doesn't grade on the curve, and we know we're not supposed to either. We wouldn't think, "I must be doing O.K. because I dress more modestly than so-and-so," or "I have more contentment than Mrs. Next Pew Over." My own sanctification will not be well served if I am busy making myself feel better by looking at the sins of others. I need to, as the saying goes, be busy about tending my own garden. While we tend to be on guard against this temptation with respect to ourselves, we strangely succumb to it with our children. We grade ourselves as parents on a curve, through the medium of our children. We determine how we are doing by comparisons and we choose comparisons that are bound to come out well for us. We go to the grocery store and see the child screaming for Sugar-Coated Sugar Bombs and we are good for a week of contentment with the way own children are growing in grace. We have confidence that we are doing better that those other families that put their children in government schools. They, after all, are losing their children. It is a pitiful thing indeed that we would use such instances to make ourselves feel better, righteous, or secure.

We need to remember our Lord's parable about the bad steward. He didn't lose his talent, he failed to multiply it. When the master returned, the steward ran and got the coin he had been given. We are called to multiply our talents in and through the gift of our children. Our goal isn't simply to get them into the kingdom, but to raise them to be heroes of the faith. I know some outwardly great men of God, who the Lord has certainly used in mighty ways in others' lives, whose children's lives are in shambles. For these men—as it was with Eli's sons—the attention was not directed in the right direction.

We rightly handle our talents when we teach our children to rightly handle their own. We need to teach them to value the right talents, as we seek to do the same. We have children who are "talented" with reading, piano, baseball, etc. But these things at which they shine and which gets the attention of others—including the heathen—are not what it's all about. Every year before baseball starts and during the season, my husband gives Campbell a lengthy speech, reminding him that he doesn't care if Campbell strikes out every time and misses every ball that's hit to him. He wants Campbell to have a gentle and quiet spirit, to be humble, to be an encouragement to his teammates and a joy to his coaches. We pray that Darby and Delaney will play the piano and violin for God's glory, and not their own.

When we read the Hall of Faith in Hebrews 11, we ought to pray that our children will be in that hall. As Gregg Harris once wrote, we don't simply want our children to be able to read and understand the great Reformers, we want them to *be* the great Reformers, for their generation. It is necessary, however, that we understand what greatness and Reformation are. That is, our talents will be best multiplied not by raising famous theologians, heroines of renown, sports stars or Christian pop singers. Our talents will be multiplied if we humbly raise up godly children who will raise up godly children. The greatness isn't in popularity and fame, not even in the "talents," but in the faithfulness.

We will assuredly answer for what we have done with the children God has given us. Indeed, we may even answer for the grandchildren He gives us. That should sober and scare us.

It should also send us running to the only One who can give us the wisdom and fortitude to endure at such a task and not just give up before we really start. Just like the stewards in the parable, we also serve a stern master, so let us with fear and trembling be busy with our calling.

CHAPTER TWO

Support and Submit

Being helpmeets to our husbands is a noble calling. Satan and worldly "wisdom" often confuse us on this issue. Because we are surrounded by false and harmful teaching on a daily basis, we often lose sight of what our goals should be in this area: primarily, respecting our husbands as instructed in Ephesians 5, and serving as co-laborers with them in building God's kingdom. While it is a role of co-laborer, it is done in a posture of submission. Let's take a look at various ways this plays out.

My Hero

I don't want to hurt your feelings, but by and large, it seems women are more relational than men. Generally speaking, relationships matter more to us—similar to how most men are interested in sports, hunting, or fishing. Our interests, of course, seem more sensible and indeed pious to us. After all, haven't we been told that Christianity is a relationship, not a religion? But there are dangers for us in our interests too. If sports can become idols to men, and rest assured that they can, can't relationships become idols for us women? Isn't it just possible that what means so much to us can mean too much to us? And which relationship is most likely to be the most important to us and fill that role of something to idolize but our relationship with our husband. This is, or at least ought to be, our closest human relationship. This is the man who knows us best, who sees us naked. If there is a general danger to idolatry among people, there is a special danger to idolatry in relationships among women, and the most potent danger to idolatry among wives.

God has called me to call my husband "lord." God has drawn a parallel between my relationship to him and my relationship to Him. That is, just as the church honors and obeys Jesus, so we are called to honor and obey our own husbands. This analogy—like all analogies—breaks down eventually. Before it does so however, it takes us rather far down this dangerous road. Our husbands, in some sense, are to be like gods to us. But our husbands, no matter how wonderful they are, are not up to the task of being God. They make great idols, which means they make awful idols. And if our husbands are Christian men it makes the temptation to idolize them that much stronger. It's pretty easy looking down our noses at the heathen, even if we're married to one. But it's also pretty easy to put a Christian husband up on a pedestal. Of course, if you find the notion of worshipping your husband too far-fetched, I hope it is your piety and not his impiety that makes it so.

How do we treat our husbands as if they were God? Let me count the ways. We expect our relationship with them to fulfill us completely when such is true only of our relationship with God. We expect them to meet all of our needs, including emotional intimacy. The modern woman may be able to bring home the bacon, fry it up in the pan, and never never let him forget he's a man, but too many modern wives expect their husbands to bring home the bacon, clean the fry pan, and never ever get to rest like a man. We expect them to always treat us like princesses, to devote their time, energy and emotions towards us. Worst of all, we expect them to be without sin. I suppose it might be somewhat normal to expect this as a newlywed, but shortly thereafter it should occur to us that we married sinners! We try to find our identity completely in our husbands when we should find our identity in Christ. We find our security in them when we ought to find our security in Christ.

Please understand, the danger in misplacing these affections of ours isn't in our husbands' heads getting too big, although I suppose this could happen. The greater danger is that we as wives would wind up angry and disappointed. Our husbands' sinful natures would be too much to bear as they would never be able to live up to the expectations we would have and we would be bitter. In the end, false gods always disappoint, even when they are the husbands we love. Suddenly, when this happens, our "gods" become human to us and we let them know how they've failed us. We rant, rave, and nag precisely because they didn't meet our expectations, though there is no way they ever could have. Then, in our further audacity we turn to the living God and complain about the god He has given us.

How do we tear down this stronghold and flee from idol worship? Before we try to lower our view of our husbands, we must first elevate our view of our Savior. That is, we must rest in our relationship with our heavenly Father, secure through our heavenly husband, Jesus. All that we long for in terms of affirmation, love, emotional intimacy—all of these are met in Jesus. We must recognize that the Lord not only *can* meet all of our needs, but that He already *has*, and *will* forever more. The woman at the well went from husband to husband in search of peace. But she didn't even recognize that the Man who asked for water could make it so she would never thirst again. We must rejoice that He is indeed without sin. We must find our identity and security in Him.

After recognizing that our husbands aren't God, we must be careful not to fall off the wagon on the other side. Our husbands are not our equals but have been placed in authority over us. Their sins do not diminish their authority. We still submit to our husbands even as we labor and worship alongside them (and no, I'm not saying we submit to all husbands, just our own). We should have a *high* view of our husbands, respecting them, honoring them, and loving them like no other person on earth—but we should have a *transcendent* view of God. He alone is our Maker. He alone sent His Son to atone for our sins. He alone has promised to remake us. Remembering this will enable us to tell them apart. And this will honor both of them, giving honor to whom honor is due, in an appropriate way.

My Husband, The Jerk

I'm allowed to tell the following story because it amuses my husband so much and because he thought it was just the right story to share in this article. A laugh this good is worth it, even if he is on the short end of the humor. Speaking with his parents about a distressing disagreement, my RC said to his father RC, "But I don't want them to think I'm a big, fat jerk." My RC's mother Vesta (who is a very sweet woman) said, "Oh, honey, they won't think you're a jerk!" Then RC Sr. replied, "Notice she didn't say anything about being big and fat!"

That said, I'm not writing this because I know what it's like to have a big, fat jerk for a husband. I am grateful that none of those things define who he is. He is, however, wrong sometimes and a sinner at all times. But I'm supposed to help him, support him, honor him, submit to him.

When confronted with the plain teaching of Ephesians 5, wives will often voice this objection: "I would be glad to submit to my husband, were he more like Jesus." But it is Jesus Himself who calls us to submit to our own imperfect husbands. In other words, a failure to submit to our sinful husbands is a failure to submit to our perfect Husband.

We need to be doubly aware of the reality of sin in the husband/wife relationship as we seek to obey our Lord. Isn't it possible, if not likely, that one reason we sometimes think our husbands are big, fat jerks is because we are big, fat jerks? Why is it that we don't trust them to be objective, wise, and reasonable in what should be done, while we fully trust ourselves to be such? Isn't it just possible that we object to them because they rightly object to something in us? We want to have things our own way and are regularly struggling to get it. We rebel against our God-given authority when he says, "No," or "No, we're not going to deal with this like that." Keep in mind, also, that many women, who would never dream of rebelling outwardly or vocally, are quite the opposite in their thought lives. If lusting after another woman in one's heart is adultery, then so is grumbling against one's husband in heart rebellion.

Then there is this other major problem: all of our husbands are sinners. Yep, every husband you know sins every single day. Even that guy who you sinfully think is so perfect, who never does anything wrong, the one you think your friend is so blessed with. He sins every day too. Not only does Jesus know that our husbands are sinners—and still He commands us to obey them—the devil knows it too. It is he who is telling us that we have been put in this untenable situation, he who whispers that there's just no way we can submit to THAT.

One way we can send the devil packing is to remember that Jesus hasn't left us without recourse if we're in a difficult marital situation. First, we are to obey God rather than men. Just as Peter would not cease preaching in Jesus' name—though commanded to do so by the Sanhedrin—so must we refuse if our husbands command us to do what God clearly forbids or forbid us to do what God clearly commands. Don't miss the "clearly" part of that statement. It is essential and doesn't allow for the wiggle room most of us would like. Obviously, every time we disagree with our husbands we think they are asking us to act unwisely. This doesn't undo the command to submit. If it's a close call, do what he says and—this is where trusting God really comes in—let him deal with the consequences. And if it's something you're really displeased about (he insisted on the Chevy van with more miles and you really wanted the Ford… it was such a pretty color) ask the Lord to help you be joyful about it. Don't sit around praying for the day when your husband will realize you were right. Instead, pray for the day when your husband can have absolute confidence that you are behind him, and will joyfully follow wherever he leads.

Secondly, we do have a court of appeals, the session of our local church. Just as our husband should appeal to the session should we fail to submit, so ought we to do the same if they fail in their obligations to us. God has given us our sessions and we should not fear to go to them.

Regardless of our situations, we still are called to honor our husbands. Even if we have a case that requires intervention by our session, we are to work to honor him. This is not a time to say, "Good, now he's finally in trouble and I can say whatever I want. I'm really going to let him have it and make sure everyone hears about it." If he really is being a big, fat jerk, we are not therefore given a green light to speak disrespectfully to and about him. If he is being a jerk, we humbly refuse to disobey God and/or humbly go to the session. Whatever the circumstances, we must remember that our Husband in heaven sees and knows all things. Our hearts—and not our husbands—are what really need to change. Ask the Lord to give you a fervor for confronting your own sin and start with ways in which you may not be honoring the man God has given you.

Tonto

It's bad enough that it begins with the language of psychology. This alone should tell us that there is something seriously wrong with the idea. The idea uses language that we don't find in God's Word. Worse still, it is psycho-babble of the feminist kind. We are told by psychological feminists of the importance of having our own "identity." We certainly are told no such thing in the Bible. In fact, the only identity we're encouraged to possess and display is that of a Christian. From the time Eve was created and stepped onto the stage of the world, she remembered (until the Fall) that she was made to be a helper for Adam. Her beloved, upon seeing her for the first time says, "This at last is bone of my bones and flesh of my flesh; she shall be called Woman, because she is taken out of the man."

Isn't it interesting how we vacillate between hungering for intimacy (which this text certainly affirms) and hungering for autonomy—which this text clearly denies. We want to be close to our husbands and we want to be our own. We can have the first, but only by giving up the second. When we recognize what we are, then we can become what we are called to be. Women were not made to be the stars of the show, but were instead made to be helpers suitable for their husbands. Men were not made to be the stars of the show either, but to show forth the glory of Christ. They, however, have a more outward calling than the woman and are leading the way in many arenas. To put it another way, women were not made to be Lone Rangers—we were made to be Tontos. We share with our husbands the call to bring down the bad guys. We share with them the call to rule well. But we do so as sidekicks, supporting cast members. Remember while digesting this last statement that Scripture also teaches that women are equally valuable, equally gifted, equally redeemed and equally loved. We are called to be helpers in this grand story of history. What an honor and blessing! It is something to thank God for—that He chooses to use us weaker vessels (as He calls us in His Word). It is not to be chafed against and resented.

This, of course, is true of the church as well. That is, she, as the second Eve, exists to help her Husband as He is about the business of finishing the story. She too is called to intimacy with her Husband. But she also often struggles with wanting an identity separate from her Husband. It sort of helps to see the foolishness of wives seeking their own glory and identity when you imagine the church, as the bride of Christ, trying to do the same thing. How absurd! What identity would the church have on its own without the Bridegroom? Silly, isn't it, when a woman is already joined to a man and blessed because of it, that she would seek to loose herself and try to do her own thing and be admired for it.

Our "glory" as women, like the church, is wrapped up not in making a name for ourselves, but making a name for our husbands under Christ. Our identity should be in him and Him. We need to learn to assess ourselves in light of this calling. We should regularly consider our lives and our relationships with our husbands, asking several important questions. Keep in mind that these are taken right from Holy Scripture. In playing my role in the story, am I acting in such a way that my husband can trust me? Am I doing him good and not harm all the days of his life? Is my husband known in the gates and does he sit among the elders of the land?

Consider the temptation for women to seek their own identities and followings on the Internet. It seems that many women attempt to make a platform for themselves and their own teaching which is quite separate from assisting their husbands in their callings. Aside from the myriad problems of setting oneself up as a teacher of others, under no ecclesiastical authority to do so (which is certainly not something only grabbed at by women), it boggles the mind to think of the time these women devote to their blogs, websites, and commenting on other sites.

Very early in my experience with cancer—while still undergoing chemotherapy and knowing that I still had to face radiation and at least one more major surgery—one of these well-meaning women called and asked me to write a book about my experience. At the time, however, I had to say as politely as I could, "If I have any energy to do anything during this time, I'm going to use it to minister to my husband and children." Various family members and friends were helping us for weeks and months at a time during that period just to keep our home running, with everyone fed, the laundry done ,and so on. The oldest of our six children was ten at the time and our youngest was one. The last thing that would have been appropriate for me to do right then would be to write a book. It is necessary for women to fight the temptation to want to make a name for themselves, even if it is only in cyberspace. And women should be very careful not to justify the time and energy they spend in such pursuits by saying that they are just helping their husbands and are doing so under his authority. Those women who truly are doing that are out there, but they are few and far between.

So we women are to play supporting roles to our husbands' lead. We should do this joyfully, as unto our heavenly Husband, knowing that we support the greatest story ever told. This is not only enough, but more than enough. What a glory and delight! We help those who model the Star and together we make known His glory in our life stories.

Let's Pray for Daddy

It's not easy being the king. As we watch the movie, *It's a Wonderful Life,* we witness the astounding level of sacrifice of George Bailey and the mounting pressure that he faces.

The bank he's worked so hard to keep running is in danger of being closed and the money he needs to help save it has been lost by his forgetful uncle. Worse still, that loss would mean, "bankruptcy, scandal and prison." George spends a good deal of time wondering if it would be better if he'd never been born. For all his goodness, George isn't up to the pressure. He doesn't realize he's going through some of the callings of a king—to die to self and to lead with courage and wisdom. In the movie, we agonize along with his loved ones as he explodes in his own home. He fusses at Zuzu's teacher about the flower, about her coat being left open on her way home from school. He fusses about the incessant piano practicing. He fusses about the little guy who keeps saying, "Excuse me." (In our family, we tend to chuckle about George's response because our Maili started saying when she was two—in the cutest little voice imaginable—"'Scuse you for what?!") George wrongly takes out the pressure he feels from work on his family.

What does the faithful wife do here? In what may be the only theologically correct moment or response in the whole film, Mary gathers the children together. She's not making excuses for what Daddy has just done. She's not telling the boys they'd better not act like Daddy when they are grown or instructing the girls not to marry a man with a temper. Instead they gather together, at Mary's instruction, to pray for George. Their response to the enormous pressure Daddy was under wasn't to undo the order of the home. Mary didn't decide that since George was handling things poorly she'd better take over for a while. The eldest son didn't decide to seize control for a bit, feeling confident he could do better than his father. Instead they went for the most potent weapon in their arsenal—they prayed.

Tending Your Garden

Whatever their circumstances, whatever their vocations, our husbands are under a great deal of pressure. Even if all is well at work, at church, in the family, they still feel the weight of leadership. And it gets even tougher when things aren't going well in even one of those spheres. Our temptation is to add to that burden by complaining. We, instead of seeking to ease the pressure, add to it. Our calling as daughters of the King is to flee that temptation by getting on our knees in prayer. We need to recognize when we feel inclined to complain and—to quote another favorite character of ours—"Nip it. Nip it in the bud." We should look for growth in our sanctification, being thankful to God when we spend less and less time even allowing ourselves to think about grumbling. For most of us women, it is a life-long endeavor to put to death that voice that encourages us to whine and complain.

The serpent went after Eve in the garden. In our homes, our husband is more likely his target. After all, as the king he wears a greater target on his back. When Satan can take out a leader or even cripple him, damage is done to the whole kingdom. The wife and children are left vulnerable, as is every other person in the king's domain. The wife should be ever on her guard to prayerfully seek God's protection and strength for her husband. She should pray specifically for him regarding the various spheres of his life, that God would protect him, make him righteous, defeat his enemies (praying through imprecatory Psalms is a great model for this), make his work fruitful, help him to be a servant leader in his home, and prosper in his work.

My husband often talks about the calling of the husband to help sanctify the wife (how's that for a weight on one's shoulders?). While we along with the children, are indeed the center of the garden, we are not the total of the garden. He is to keep us, but also to go forth and gardenize the jungle. If there is a struggle going on in the latter, the last thing we ought to be doing is discouraging him by showing our propensity to complain. Far less should we determine that all will be made well if we just point out his weaknesses.

Although all Christians are called to encourage all other Christians to righteousness, there is no corresponding call on the woman to sanctify her husband, in the same sense that the husband is called to labor for the sanctification of his wife. However, while we are not responsible for him in the same sense that he is for us, if we are wise we should long for nothing more than to see our husbands grow in grace. If we would seek to fulfill our calling to be a help to our husbands, should we not seek to help where it matters the most? There is nothing more important that we as wives can do for our husbands than to pray that they would grow in grace. If we are wise, we would encourage the children to do the same. This is the kind of help we were created to provide. What a gift and what a delight! If you want a wonderful life, pray without ceasing and believe the promises of God.

CHAPTER THREE

Sanctification in Child Training

While men, and especially husbands, are primarily responsible within the family to oversee child training and encourage sanctification in the wife and children, much of the daily work involved with it is the woman's responsibility. Because we have the delightful task of being with them for much of the day, we are attuned to needs our children have in regard to training (even if this involves basic life skills) and instruction in righteousness. This can be a complicated task, but with God's grace and wisdom, one that is truly a blessing.

Good Prophets in Skirts

There is a sense in which all followers of Christ need to be prophets, not exactly like in the Bible—directly speaking God's revealed words to His people—but in bringing the Word of God to bear in people's lives. While we are not at all egalitarian about men's and women's roles, we need not be afraid of affirming that women are also called to be prophets. All of us are to be prophets as Christians. The question is: To whom are we to be prophetic?

The very purpose of having authority over another is so that the Word of God can be brought to bear. When God places us—under our husband's authority—as authorities in the lives of our children, this means we are to proclaim the Word to them, washing them with it. All of us as Christians should be working on our sanctification, striving with the Holy Spirit's help to be more like Christ. When we have authority over someone, as husbands do with wives or as parents do with children, we are responsible for proclaiming God's Word to those loved ones, helping them to see what God has in mind when He tells us to be imitators of Christ.

We sometimes are tempted to mold our daughters into our own image, rather than the image of Christ. There's nothing wrong with our daughters enjoying the same things we do, whether it's music or cross-stitch, art or cooking. However, this should not be our goal. We shouldn't be striving to make them into a junior "us." We want to see our daughters become women of God and our sons men of God—mighty warriors in His kingdom, more righteous than we. We should be ever vigilant in keeping that as our goal. Not in the sense of trying to hurry them through growing up, but in having the end result that God desires ever before us. The means to the end of raising godly seed is the application of the Word to our children's lives.

How do you apply the Word? First, under your husband's authority, the Bible must be the center, the foundation, the beginning and the end of your homeschool. That doesn't mean that every single math problem has to have the explanation that, "This is orderly, sensible and the same every time because God is orderly, logical and immutable." Such, however, should be central in their thinking because you have talked about it regularly and have that understanding as the basis for all they are learning. Talk regularly about your desire for them to read well so that they can read and understand God's Word for themselves. When you pray each day before you give them their lessons, you can ask God to help the children do their best for God's glory and so that they can continually learn to know, love, and serve Him better. Isn't this the purpose for which we are teaching them at home in the first place?

Secondly, God's Word needs to be spoken in the context of discipline. Every time we discipline one of our children, we need to remind him in prayer and instruction that God's Word requires discipline for disobedience; that the child might be conformed to the image of Christ, learning to repent of sin and desiring reconciliation with the one offended and with Christ. You need to help him understand, through consistency, lack of anger, and verbal reminders that you are not disciplining him because his screaming hissy fit got on your nerves, but because God's Word says we are to do all things without grumbling or complaining. We would all do well to remember that discipline is not just for times of correction, but for times of encouragement and edification. We need to speak weal to them, as well as woe. We don't say, "I'm so glad you didn't throw a hissy fit because you know that gets on my nerves." Instead try, "We are called in the Bible to have a gentle and quiet spirit and I'm grateful to God when you show forth that trait, as you did this afternoon." Especially with traits that you as their mother know are not their strong points or that they've been working on, it is important to verbally tell them when you notice them doing the right thing. What an encouragement and sign of love to them when they know that both God and Mom and Dad notice!

Third, the Word must be central to your conversation, which means you need to be spending lots of time in it yourself. When we look at the stars we need to remind our children—even if they are too little or incapacitated to understand—that the heavens declare the glory of God. I remember when our daughter, Delaney, was learning the first few questions of the catechism, she would regularly say something like, "God made me! And He made that tulip, and the slide, and my baby doll!" What a terrific thing when our children learn through God's Word about His world and His wonderful care for them. We have found several sources to be helpful in school time and during family worship for memorizing Scripture: they are *For Instruction in Righteousness* by Doorposts and the *Memlock* Bible memory system.

It may sound strange, but you can also decorate with Scripture—from framed prints of verses to cards you've written out and posted in conspicuous places for your family's edification. It's difficult for me to be upset while washing dishes when I look up and see my index card that says, "A merry heart makes a cheerful countenance, but by sorrow of the heart the spirit is broken" (Proverbs 15:13).

We need to remember, as with the prophets in Scripture, that we are to speak the words and the wisdom God has given us, not our own thoughts and guesses. And when we do this, we do not speak with timidity. We are not being feminine when we sprinkle with the Word rather than scrubbing with it. We are to be bold as the prophets of old.

Water

It is a perennial temptation for many of us to be more concerned with appearances than with reality. This temptation dates back to the Fall. Adam and Eve didn't seek to cover their sin or the evil in their hearts; they sought to cover their nakedness. And if Eve is anything like her descendants, she was probably worried that God might notice that the clothes she made weren't clean.

This temptation to be concerned with appearances also applies to how we view our children. As moms, we are tempted to be more concerned with what others think of our children than what God does. Or we worry that others won't notice certain strengths and graces that the Lord has bestowed on our children (through no deservedness of our own). God knows the reality of our children's hearts, sanctification, and diligence, while others know only the image. We want our children to be thought of as clean-cut and on the straight and narrow—which is rather a different thing from holiness, righteousness, godliness, and bearing much of the Fruit of the Spirit.

Of course, if we are tempted to dwell on appearances in regards to our children, we are tempted to do the same with ourselves. We want to have a good reputation and for others to think highly of us—often more than we want to do well. This may be why God gave us our husbands. God tells them to make sure that we are washed in the water of the Word (Ephesians 5:26). What cleanses us isn't the right detergent at the grocery store but the Word of God.

Though the text doesn't say this directly, it isn't a stretch to suggest that we have the same calling with respect to our children. As we seek to help our children grow in grace, the best thing we can do for them is to wash them with the water of the Word. What a comfort that is—the Bible is sufficient for all of life. If I immerse my children in it as God instructs, things will go well for them generally, and they will have the wisdom they need from God's hand. Another good thing to remember is that I don't need to be concerned about every wind of child-care doctrine that comes along. I know that anything that goes against or doesn't acknowledge Scripture in child training is a waste of my reading time. This means I'm not damaging them by continually changing my tack and jumping from one way of doing things to another. God's Word grounds our family and gives us the security He intends for us to have.

Immersing our children in God's Word means there are plenty of formal means of "taking baths." That is, our homeschooling studies should be suffused with teaching from the Bible. We should be constantly bringing in Scripture references as they relate to whatever we are currently studying. Bathing them in God's Word also helps us establish our children's own faithful habits of Bible reading. We should teach them to love the Word of God and to regularly read it. Along with Bible reading, they should be encouraged in their Scripture memorization. That's a great thing to do together as a family (under your husband's direction if he so desires). We have been humbled and blessed to have our commitment to family worship translate into our learning more Bible verses than we ever had before. It's a great thing when the Lord helps us to learn along with our children.

The Bible ought to also be part of our ordinary conversations with our children—not just during "formal" school time or during devotions or family worship. There are numerous opportunities each day to bring the Word of

God to bear in our children's lives. When one of our blessings grumbles against another, they might hear me ask if they would like to be grumbled against in that way. If they grumble back a "No," we talk about what the Bible says about doing unto others. When they see their Daddy being persecuted for righteousness' sake by former friends who are supposed to be brothers and sisters in Christ, we talk about what love among the brethren should look like. We will also talk to them about God supplying all our needs and about the fact that we are blessed when we are persecuted and when others revile and speak all manner of ill against us. We can be assured that these lessons will stick with our children for life.

Even when we as parents repent we must wash them with the water of the Word. That is, if I lose my temper and apologize—sincerely asking them to forgive me and not being afraid to do so just because I'm the parent, I should also remind them, "The Bible says a soft answer turns away wrath and I didn't give a soft answer, did I?" Show them, whenever you can, that Scripture applies to all of us. When they see you wash yourself with the Word imagine the lifelong impact this will make on them and your future grandchildren!

This should remind us that we cannot wash them with the Word of God if we ourselves are dry. We must drink deeply, by immersing ourselves and being washed by this potent and cleansing water, remembering that it and He are making each of us into a spotless bride.

Spirit Fed

As Christians, we do not take seriously enough the promise of the coming of the Holy Spirit. We should be clued in when we read of Jesus telling the disciples that it was better for them that He should go, that He might send the Spirit. If we bother to give this any thought at all, we think in theological terms. That is, we think this promise is for the church, or for adults. We don't often think about how this might influence our calling to raise up godly seed. We miss that this promise is for us *and* for our children.

For too long we have thought about the relationship between the new covenant and our children as being an issue about baptism. That is, we are content to debate over whether the new covenant is only made with actual believers, or if it is made only with those who verbally profess belief. In reality, it's an issue about the baptism of the Holy Spirit. That is to say, in the new covenant, all true believers are empowered and indwelt by the Spirit and if our children have been born again, then they too have been empowered and indwelt by the Holy Spirit. The issue is less water baptism, more Spirit baptism.

This means that we are not merely training our children to be more obedient, but are cultivating in them the fruit of the Spirit as found in Galatians 5:22-23. We are not merely looking for them to conform to an outward standard of obedience—we are striving to see that they are made more like Jesus, through the work of His Spirit. This is the "new and improved" we are seeking in and for them. We have confidence that it will come to pass and can train them because we too are grateful for the gift of the Spirit. The same Spirit that indwells us that we might be faithful parents indwells them that they might be faithful children.

This new covenant should first affect how we pray for our children. We should be praying that they would grow in grace, that they would bear much fruit, and that they would become more effective soldiers in the kingdom. Praying for an increase in godly character, for wisdom and fortitude to do that which is pleasing in God's sight. We are praying for them, not for our own relief in dealing with their sin. Our prayers for them are not disguised prayers for ourselves, "Oh Lord, please help little Susie learn to stop that annoying screeching she always does. It drives me crazy!" Instead we are praying that Susie would be given a more gentle and quiet spirit. There is a big difference.

Secondly, the new covenant affects the confidence with which we pray. The God we are praying to is the same God who indwells these children. He has promised to not only forgive their sins, but to cleanse them from all unrighteousness. We ought not grow weary or be discouraged. In believing that God can do great things in our children, it is easy to get frustrated, fearing that He isn't. This is especially true when we see areas of struggle in our children that must be dealt with repeatedly. Sometimes we think they are making no progress and fear that they never will. However, the fact that they don't make their beds after repeated reminders and consequences probably doesn't mean they're not saved. We need to remember the areas where we repeatedly struggle, remembering that the struggles may well be a sign of the indwelling of the Holy Spirit. A conversation I had many years ago with my father-in-law made a deep impression on me and has come to mind often. He impressed upon me that concern about one's salvation is a good thing. If one wasn't saved, he usually wouldn't be concerned about it.

Third, this new covenant affects the way that we pray. We ought to be leading and modeling how to pray for these Spirit-indwelt little ones. Are we always praying for sick loved ones and for the Lord's blessing on our husband's work (which are both very good things for which to pray), but neglecting to pray for our children's and our own growth in becoming more like Jesus? Are we remembering to praise God privately and in our children's presence for the areas that He is conforming us to His own image? Do we remember in our praise to specifically focus on the fruit of the Spirit that He is manifesting? Or do we focus mainly on asking Him to heal a broken bone or thank Him only for the ice cream that we enjoyed at the picnic? These are good things to bring before the Lord in prayer also—especially if the children are mentioning them—but they should not be the focus of how we are teaching them to pray. I have always appreciated how my husband will gently add on to the little ones' prayer requests, saying something like, "And how about if Daddy also prays that the Lord would give you more patience with your sister when the two of you are cleaning up your room?" This kind of leading teaches the children that the Lord cares about our daily circumstances and the health of our physical bodies and so on, but He also cares about our spiritual maturity and has given us a Comforter to encourage us on to holiness.

While we are looking for improvements in our children's righteousness, studying to see how their fruit is coming along, let us also look for improvement in our families. Let us remember to thank God that our children are more spiritually mature than we were at their age. Let us pray and teach them to pray—while they are still young, that their children will surpass us all. Let us pray for progressive familial sanctification, for this is a mighty way that the kingdom grows.

Suffer the Children

As parents raising covenant children for the glory of God, indeed, as covenant children living in the tension of the already and the not yet, so much of our work involves that virtue that stands *contra mundum* like few others—delayed gratification. If we are to succeed as parents, we need to look to the long-term goal, not just to keeping the kids from making a mess in the kitchen or keeping the restless natives somewhat corralled. We are working toward the goal of our children becoming godly men and women. That doesn't mean, however, that all our lives or all their young lives are only good for building the future. That is, we want them to be godly boys and godly girls, not boys and girls in training who are merely waiting to be godly adults. This has a profound impact on how we see them in relationship to the church.

Most of us understand that the "catholic" in the Apostles' Creed refers to the universal church. We are not to buy into schemes that divide the church, that see the church in other countries as separate from the church here (speaking, of course, of legitimate, true churches). Shouldn't this idea of "catholic" also apply to our children? We are one church when we meet for Lord's Day worship, not an adult's church and a children's church. And so we ought to go together as families into the corporate worship of Christ. As we do this it is not as training for our children's future, but as obedience in our children's present.

As we seek to be obedient in worshiping with our children and not sending them off to make a craft somewhere else in the church building, we need to encourage them to sing and to say what we are singing and saying and to pray when we are praying. I have to remind myself especially with my children who are four and under that they need to not be lying down on the pew or coloring or trying to get the baby to laugh when the rest of us are singing the Apostles' Creed. They can sing too! And sing joyfully, with all their might, unto the Lord. What destroys worship is not something unique to youth, but something common to us all: Sin. They are, we presume, redeemed sinners. They, like we, must celebrate His grace. They, like we, must mourn their sin. They, like we, must look to the consummation of the kingdom. And we, like they, ought to be memorizing Bible verses and learning the catechism. Our children are not trainees, but worshipers now. They will not make it on the basis of our faith, but on their own. Therefore, let them live now in that faith.

It's ironic really when we look at our children as incapable of understanding or participating in worship. There are very few other things from which we hold them back, yet nothing is more important to their growth and obedience. For most of our children, we wouldn't dream of delaying their potty training or learning to ride a bike or learning to read. Yet we make all sorts of excuses, verbally or in our heads, about why they can't possibly worship in "big church." Yes, it's more difficult keeping an eye on them, rebuking them for irreverent behavior, and not being able to pay as close attention to the sermon as we would like. But wouldn't you much rather take seriously God's instruction to "suffer the little children to come unto me"(Mark 10:14) and hear the sounds that come "out of the mouths of children and tiny, nursing babes"(Psalm 8:2) as they bring forth God-ordained praises? And won't you delight when they are six or seven and they are even more self-consciously and actively participating, opening their Bibles to the designated passage and so on, already having experienced and enjoyed six or seven years of corporate worship?!

Since our children are part of our family and part of God's family, in order for them to understand the necessity of corporate worship, we must teach them the glories of our book, the Bible. We are the family of God, Abraham's sons and daughters, from our eight-year-old down to our four month old. The Old Testament is important for them to know, so they can know their great God, so that they can know the family story, so that they can know who they are and where they have come from. The Old Testament does not exist as an excuse for flannel graphs, as fun and helpful as they might be. Neither is the Old Testament a collection of stories designed to teach the children the importance of telling the truth or of being brave, or why it's not nice to call some other kid a cheese-headed bean-boy. Instead it is our family story, the very identity of what we and our children are.

They are not too immature for the things of God, but are to be raised in the nurture and admonition of the Lord. God didn't put an "age of accountability" onto that requirement. We can assume that the time during which we are to raise our children in the nurture of the Lord includes their whole lives under our roofs. In light of this, we must not see them as only our children, but as children of the King—heirs and recipients of the promise of the indwelling Spirit. Seek to be faithful now in having your children worship the King with you. You are training them to be more active participants in worship, but you are also beseeching the Holy Spirit to accept your children's "morning sacrifice of praise and thanksgiving" every Lord's Day. They can do it now. Obey

God and let them. Rejoice in His faithfulness now and into the future.

In Due Time

One of the great things about being a keeper at home is that you never run out of work. For most of us, we can't recall many times, if any, where we sat around thinking, "Well, you know, I've got this time on my hands. Wonder what I should do now." Despite the fact that we have much worthwhile work to occupy our days, one of the most discouraging things is that we often feel we never actually finish a job. Yes, when you paint the outside of your house, it will need to be painted again one day. And laundry has an even shorter shelf-life. Raising our children is at the core of our calling of being keepers at home. We delight to know that we have important work to do—seeing our children grow in grace. We are wise to remember that this is central to what we're called to do. But we can also become easily discouraged, for our children remain sinners.

We can face in our children the same paradox we face in ourselves. The more righteous we become, the more we become aware of our sin. That is, as we progress, we see that we have farther to go. The same can happen with our children. In fact, it should. We need to be careful not to be satisfied with doing better than the heathen. We should always be looking carefully at our children's fruit and seeing where praise is due and where pruning needs to be done. Discouragement often comes when we see the sinful parts of our children, some of which are very obvious because they are repetitive offenses and/or because they are particularly ugly. All of this is more reason for us to long for the return of the King.

As with ourselves, our children will only be perfect when they die, or when He returns. This is something we ought to look for with joyful hope (not their dying—but their being made perfectly righteous). In fact, we should work especially hard at remembering this. It is easy to look in hope for our daughter Shannon to be made whole—that she will talk, sing, and pray, praising God in her perfect little whole self. Jesus will feed her at the marriage feast of the Lamb and she will eat whatever is offered because she will be well. But what really ails her–though it's not so physically noticeable in our other children–is the same thing that ails us all. The problem isn't her brain, but her sinful heart. We all have the same condition and it is a congenital defect. All the children we have will be born the same way and we as parents are likewise afflicted. There is no way to avoid it, but there are certain things that can be done. We can also rest assured that if we belong to the Lord, we will get progressively "better" until we die.

As we look forward in hope, we must look forward with patience. This is difficult because we want what we want and we want it NOW. But God does what He does in His time, not ours. You would think that after the umpteenth time of our looking back and seeing that God's timing was perfect in a situation that we would at least realize that God knows what He's doing—and that we should be ashamed of ourselves for not taking Him at His Word. This confidence in God's timing being perfect should also give us perfect peace about the day-to-day disruptions and aggravations that often leave us frustrated. When the three-year-old spills her milk for the 20th time or someone forgets to say " please" although she's heard the reminder her whole life, we can bear it with patience. We discipline where needed, looking to see if the reins need to be tightened, do it, and move on—cheerfully. We should keep in mind as we look at our children that we too are children. We should be striving to love our children as our heavenly Father loves us, with patience and perseverance. We must remember from God's Word that His love never fails. If I am to be like Christ to my children, I need to love them faithfully. This means looking past my own selfish desires for comfort and ease and loving them sacrificially. If I'm reading on the couch or talking to a friend on the phone, I don't want to be interrupted because Maili needs her teeth brushed or Delaney needs help with the breakfast dishes. But sacrificial love means not only giving up my "free" time, it also means I do it joyfully, being grateful that God has given us Maili and Delaney. It also means recognizing that sometimes (often times) loving and nurturing them involves mundane things that I would rather not have to do. Training children in the nurture and admonition of the Lord involves huge things such as discipline, teaching Scripture, encouraging them to serve others and so on, but it also involves Mommy just being there with them, getting them up and dressing and feeding them. Lots of these things can be done by someone else and can sometimes be done by others with no harm to the children, but Mommy also needs to be regularly pouring herself into her children by doing these things for them in love. Our older children are certainly trained and capable of doing much to help, but I am still responsible for many small tasks in taking care of our family.

Few things will help our little ones grow in grace more than seeing our hopeful expectancy. As we pray for Jesus' return, we show them where our hope is. We show them that we are here for His kingdom and that everything we do should bear witness to this fact. We are not here for our own ends. Most importantly, we show them that we seek to be stewards of our children, knowing that they are really His.

Spilled Milk

With seven children, we buy a lot of milk—some from the grocery store and some fresh from the farm. Though we are getting away from drinking it at every meal, we still usually go through at least six gallons a week. We do not, however, get the maximum caloric benefit from every drop we buy. Some of it ends up consumed by dish towels and Bounty "quicker-picker-uppers". That is to say, we also have our fair share of spilled milk. What follows after each spill is not only the work of cleaning it up, but understanding how it came to pass. When milk gets spilled, we have to go through the struggle of determining whether it stemmed from youthfulness or from sinfulness. Was it simply little hands, or was it little sinful hands? And while we're busy figuring this out, we must make sure to keep our own hands from sin.

Some parents are too quick to excuse sin on the basis of youth. "Little Jimmy didn't lie. He's too little to understand the difference between a lie and the truth. One day he'll learn the difference, but for now, we'll just have to let it go." Never mind that little Jimmy is four or five years old and goes through various verbal sparring matches with his siblings every day. Never mind that if we tell him, "Henceforth, you will be permitted to eat only ice cream and donuts," that he will not believe us. Here it is not Jimmy but Jimmy's parents who can't distinguish between the truth and the lie.

Other parents fall off the other side of the glass of milk. They hold to the W.C. Fields theory of children. They seem to believe that being a minor is a sin in itself. They're either trying to make their children grow up too fast or have no enjoyment and patience with their children when they are little. And when childishness rears its little head in these homes, soon anger rears its ugly head.

As is so often the case, in determining whether an action is sinful foolishness or age-appropriate childishness, the tool for figuring it out is as simple and as complex as wisdom. We have already made some progress when we remember after one of these incidents simply to ask the question—which one of these is the source of the problem? If we ask the question, we will usually have little trouble discerning the answer. Sometimes our children get disciplined for spilling milk and sometimes they do not. If we are doing well, the difference is in their behavior and not our mood at the moment. In other words, if the refrigerator door broke, we had fourteen phone calls and Socks the outside dog has decided to come inside, I don't fly off the handle if Erin Claire drops a big bowl of soup because Socks runs in front of her. If she decides, on the other hand, to carry the soup to the table when I told her not to, that is an offence that needs to be disciplined because it is disobedience. If, on the third hand, the child is trying to balance his milk cup on his nose, he will soon have difficulty sitting in his chair. This is sinful foolishness. In asking for trouble, the child is asking for discipline. But if the child was simply passing the potatoes, we will pass on the spanking.

Our goal for the children is both that they would mature and that they would become more godly. That is, just as Jesus did, we want them to grow in wisdom and in stature. Critical to getting this done is to encourage them to want to do the same. Let them know what your goals are for them. Let them know that you want them to get to the point where they can say, "I'm not doing "x" even though it looks like fun, because I know that is foolishness and that's not pleasing to God."

While it may be hard to see them grow up so fast (Darby groans when I pull out her old clothes for her little sisters and then get all misty-eyed!) we want them to delight in this. We want our children to grow into adulthood. It is a gradual process, of course, but we should see progress all along the way. They can't say, "When I was a child, I spoke as a child..." if they have never put away childish things. Silly voices, sucked thumbs, and special blankets all have their places. But what was once cute is unbecoming when it is no longer appropriate for a maturing young person.

Therefore, let us push to maturity; not as in some desperate race, but in wisdom. We don't want our young ladies to be more comfortable with a baby doll than with a baby. We don't want our young men wearing silly caps like school boys. If their idea of a grand evening is hours upon hours of video games, then they still have much growing to do, no matter what their age or how hard they might have worked that day. Say Yes to joy, child-like faith, and child-like exuberance. But that child-like faith leads us, and the children we have been given, into adulthood. Let us push on in our own spiritual growth, not only seeking to raise our children for God's glory, but in pursuing wisdom in all areas of our lives.

Pressing On

You cannot be as unusual as we are without others noticing. We can't help but hear the comments. We homeschool because we believe this is right. We receive God's blessings with joy because we believe this is right. We seek to submit to our own husbands as to the Lord because we believe this is right. Which must mean, as much as we might like to pretend otherwise, that we also believe that those who do not believe as we do are wrong. Assuming we're actually right about these issues, does this mean that the devil leaves us alone, that he can't find a foothold with us? Is our right thinking—and somewhat right doing—a perfect hedge against him and his temptations? Or could it be that while we are right about education, we are wrong about gossip? Could it be that while we are right about children as blessings, we are wrong about contentedness? Could it be that while we are right about submitting to our husbands, we are wrong about honoring them? Could it be that the devil has thought of more ways of sinning than we ever dreamed were possible?

Or, could it be that while we are right about these things, we aren't right enough? How easy it is for us to wear these convictions as badges of honor, and to be content with our level of obedience. Which is why we too are called to walk the second mile. We have an obligation to not only fight the good fight, but to fight the temptation to believe that we can take a rest. After all, how many diapers have we changed? How many loads of laundry have we done? How many spills have we cleaned up?

Part of our challenge is that we see much more than just another mile ahead of us. We have yet more diapers to change and more dishes to wash, as far as our eyes can see. In the same way, when we look at how far we really have to go to be like Jesus, we realize that a mile won't get us there, not by a mile. Though we are sisters, Paul's admonition applies to us as well: "For we hear that some among you walk in idleness, not busy at work, but busybodies. Now such persons we command and encourage in the Lord Jesus Christ to do their work quietly...As for you brothers, do not grow weary in doing good" (2 Thessalonians 3:11-13). Isn't it just like Paul to discourage us from doing what we, in our fallen natures, are so prone to do?

Elisabeth Elliott has been gifted with all manner of wisdom. I am grateful for all that I have received from her. But I don't know if there was any insight, any inspiring message that has been before me so much as this simple truth: "Do the next thing." It applies to the jobs we face as keepers at home, as the mothers of our children. When we feel overwhelmed with our "to do" lists, Mrs. Elliott reminds us that the list isn't there to make us stop working, but to tell us what to do next. This same principle applies to our sanctification. If you can't put to death, at present, that grumbling and complaining spirit, perhaps you can at least keep from grumbling and complaining about that. If you haven't yet managed to not only call your husband Lord, but to see him that way in your heart, at least, the next time you speak to him, speak to him with respect. The second mile, in other words, will always be there for you. After you run it, you discover that there is still another one to go. We'll get there when tomorrow comes.

Of course, there is nothing wrong with looking back at the ground we've covered. We ought to celebrate God's grace in our lives. Milemarkers, like birthdays or anniversaries, are great times to reflect on what we have learned over the years, especially those decade-marking birthdays. The danger is that when we are looking backward, we are not moving forward. It is because God has been good, however, that we can be so confident that He will continue to be good. We can run the second mile, in other words, only as we discover that He not only will carry us along, but that He was the One that carried us for the first mile. He has begun a good work in us, and He will carry it through to the end.

Raising Up Blessings

The folks at the grocery store weren't the only ones who got bug-eyed when they saw our family. Even we were a little shocked at how close our children were in age. God opens and closes the womb. He knows the best way to "space" the children. And He, in His grace, brought them to us—at least in our early years—fast and furious. We were somewhat surprised when the Lord blessed us with six children in eight years. Now, with the addition of our baby Reilly, we are shocked in a different way. What we can't seem to fathom is the gap between him and Maili, who is now three. Two months ago, Maili was our baby girl. She is now fourth assistant. But this gap is nowhere more evident than in the children's varying abilities. Bringing home our seventh child was nothing like bringing home our first six. It is vastly different because this time we have so many helpers who are an actual help.

It may be, in contemplating this issue of maturity, that having a baby frees us from the temptation of trying to keep our children young. That is, first, we could use their help. Second, we have a young one, and so are enabled to allow the others to grow. That is, I don't feel the need for my three- and five-year-olds to remain my babies.

It is important to realize that growing up isn't just something that happens, it must be encouraged deliberately. We all can think of people who, maturity-wise, are little children in adult bodies. Sometimes we find these people in the strangest places, like in the mirror. The world around us wants to have our children "mature," but what they want is more grown-up appetites that demand to be filled right now—whether in regard to things, entertainment, or food. Things they deem for "mature" audiences, more often than not, are more puerile than that which is deemed appropriate for children only. An important part of what we Christians should desire in regard to maturity—in contrast with the world—is the ability to postpone gratification of desires. This means that we are not just helping the older ones to mature, but the little ones as well. Whether they are big or little, whether they are parents or children, we all have plenty of room to mature.

This means, of course, that even our most immature child is being trained each day to be more mature than he was the day before. Reilly, when we do not respond to each little cry by sticking a bottle in his mouth, is learning a small measure of self-control. Maili, when she is required to pick up after herself, is learning that we work first and play later. When Erin Claire holds and feeds the baby, she is learning that we are called to serve others and not just ourselves. Delaney, when she mops the unusually dirty kitchen floor, is learning that there are consequences to her actions and those of her siblings when they eat in a sloppy way. Shannon, when she isn't given a balloon every time by the folks at the grocery store, is learning that ancient wisdom: you can't always get what you want. Campbell, when he stacks firewood, though he enjoys it, is also learning that there is an important relationship between labor and provision and that stacking now, while the sun shines, helps our home to be warm in the winter. Darby, when she serves as my first assistant and right-hand young lady, learns an awful lot about being a keeper at home. My husband has been teaching us in family worship about the Fourth Commandment and that the flip side of resting on the Sabbath is that we are to be hard at work the other six days.

While we are raising our daughters to be keepers at home, we do not raise them to keep them in our homes. While we are raising our sons to remember that the home is the center of the garden, we are raising them to have gardens of their own one day. We hope they—both boys and girls—can be of help to other young families and Lord willing, we are preparing them for their own homes one day.

Maturity then isn't measured by the sophistication of the movies they watch or what books we feel they are equipped to handle. Instead it is measured by the fruit of the Spirit that they bear. This is why the center of our calling in raising them is to prune away the dead branches and to encourage the growth of much fruit. It is helpful for all of us to keep in mind the list of virtues in Galatians 5:22-23. We should keep in mind the goal of encouraging self-motivation in them. We want them to learn to strive for these things themselves. That can sometimes feel like an ongoing battle, but we know that the Spirit is certainly capable of accomplishing this. We need to work and pray toward this end and not grow weary when we don't see much fruit or progress. Take the time today to look into each of your children's eyes. Remember as you do that they will one day be adults. Then pray that when that happens they will rise up and call you blessed. If they do, it will be because—by God's grace and strength—you raised them in the nurture and admonition of the Lord and worked to make them wise and mature.

A Monkey's Uncle

We would be wise to remember that the serpent is more crafty than any of the beasts of the field. He hasn't changed, nor has he evolved. While we're busy dodging his right hook, he may just be slipping us a mickey. While we're looking in our drink for fizzy stuff, he may just bop us over the head. We have not, for instance, purged Darwin from our minds simply because we reject macroevolution. We ought, of course, to reject such foolishness. But we would be fools indeed if we think we have won the whole war when we win this one skirmish. We have not purged Darwinism from our minds, even if we can give a cogent defense against macroevolution. Darwinism is a worldview that affects not just the origin of our species, but many things related to its growth and development. Children, in this view—even if we affirm that they descend from Adam—evolve rather than mature. They pass through a series of stages in development as individuals, in much the same way man moved from *homo erectus* to *homo sapien*. If we were wise, we would shed this folly from our thinking.

Another way Darwinism affects our thinking is when we excuse sin because of the supposed inevitability of these stages. When Darby was a baby, and a very agreeable one at that, certain cynics would intone seriously, "Just wait until she turns two. Then tell me if you're enjoying life anymore." It is disturbing that many folks, even in Christian circles, assume that the so-called Terrible Twos are an inevitable part of being a child. Where in Scripture does it mention anything about this? Does it say to spare the rod and spoil the child—except when he's two, because you just can't do anything about that "stage," so don't even try. It is pitiable to see parents putting up with sin and everyone being miserable in the process just because they have adopted this worldly view of childrearing. It seems that this has become a normal stage for parents more so than a "normal" stage for children because many parents simply expect it to happen and feel as if their hands are tied. It is only "normal" insofar as sin is normal. The only thing terrible about being two is that two year olds have indeed descended from Adam, and so are sinners, as they were at one year and as they will be at three years. The only solution at all ages is to repent and believe the gospel.

Far worse than the expectation of the Terrible Twos is the common notion that teenage rebellion is a normal process in the development of children. Really? Again, where in Scripture do we see that idea espoused? Doesn't everything about maturation and development speak of seeking wisdom, not being foolish, pursuing righteousness, rejecting milk, and seeking meat as we grow in maturity? Where does the Lord in Holy Writ instruct us as Christian parents to throw up our hands when our children turn thirteen? Yet we are encouraged by Christian "psychologists" to expect this rebellion and to simply accept it. Some parents have been so heavily indoctrinated to expect this, that they actually worry if their child somehow misses it. If, indeed, rebellion is "normal," a part of the process, I suppose we ought to worry if this stage is missed.

The biblical view, however, is much different. Our children do not simply develop, progress, or evolve, going through an unavoidable set of stages that can't be changed or influenced. Rather, our children are to grow in grace. The movement isn't simply from less sophisticated to more sophisticated, but from less obedient to more obedient, less righteous to more righteous. We do not leave evolutionary baggage behind as we "evolve." We leave sin and folly behind as we drive it away with the use of the rod, with prayer, and with instruction in righteousness. We are to set patterns for our children and we are promised that those patterns, by God's grace, will last their whole lives: Teach a child the way in which he should go and when he is old he will not depart from it (Proverbs 22:6).

We, and our children, will certainly change dramatically over the course of our lifetimes. But we are not evolving from ape to man. Instead we are moving from sinners to saints, becoming more and more like Christ. This is what we are striving toward, by God's mercy and because of His love for us. What brings about this change isn't evolution, but faithful laboring in obedience, a tool given to us by God, to be used for God's ends. Our faithful labor includes washing our children with the Word and seeking to daily apply it to all of our family's lives. It includes modeling service to our King. It also includes beholding His body in the church. Then we are helping our children to become what they are meant to be—like Jesus. Then when they see Him as He is on that great day, they will be like Him.

Mama's Little Angels

As parents, most of us find it all too easy to grade on a curve. As sinners, we not only like to grade on the curve, but we like to determine its parameters. We grade ourselves and our children the same way. One of the enduring problems with grading on a curve is that the curve can change so rapidly. When we take our children to see a play at the local theater, which we do with some regularity, we can be confident that there will be government school children there to make our children look like cherubs. Even a trip to the grocery store can fill us with pride, since our children don't scream their way to getting a box of Sugar Frosted Sugar Bombs for their morning meals. It has even been known to happen that our own children become aghast at their peers, telling us as we roll down the grocery store aisle, "I think that child needs a spanking." On the flip side, we attended a Family Camp this past summer where suddenly we were surrounded by outstanding children. The standard had changed, and we found ourselves rather far down on that particular curve. The children we met at camp were, of course, a delight to be around. Better still, several of them had a positive impact on our children. But the best part may well be that it reminded us how easy it is to grade on a curve constructed for our own advantage.

The danger in the first scenario is that we can be too easily satisfied. There is, however, a corresponding danger from the other side. The danger in the second is that we can be too easily discouraged. We can become despondent if our children haven't reached the same level of spiritual maturity of those around them. The Bible promises that those who have been regenerated by the Holy Spirit are in turn indwelt by the

Holy Spirit. This is therefore a promise that we will all grow in grace. We will all—adults and children alike—become more and more like Jesus. We know that if we are truly elect, there will be more and more fruit of the Spirit that is displayed in our lives for God's glory.

What the Bible doesn't promise is that we all start the race in the same place. People are saved at different points in their lives and are going through different circumstances. Folks also run the race at different paces. What the Lord chooses to teach you through His Word and divinely appointed events, is different from how and when He teaches me. I pray that we are all regularly and soberly reminded to not presume to decide what our brothers and sisters should be experiencing as far as their sanctification. We ought to be judging those whom we are called to love with a judgment of charity.

Some of us, and even some of our children, are running the race while carrying a great deal of baggage. Depending how much time we've spent in and of the world—sometimes due to circumstances beyond our control—we can have quite a bit to overcome. Much prayer and begging the Lord for His mercy and wisdom is helpful in these situations. We can and should pray, not only that we will drop that baggage, but that our children and grandchildren might not be burdened with the same baggage.

Regardless of our circumstances and what stage we are at when beginning the race, all of us are indeed running the race. We should have before us two standards at all times—where we are coming from and where we are going. Even within the small circle of our own home we have children starting in different places. Some of our children are more naturally compliant than others. They are more easily led and are just as happy to do as asked than not. Some of them consciously choose to be as sweet and agreeable as possible, not out of fear of discipline, but out of love. Some of our children wilt under a stern word, while others consider it a challenge to not cry when being disciplined. Whatever their dispositions, each one is running a race. The finish line is complete sanctification, when we are with Christ and like Christ.

Our goal for them, and for ourselves, isn't to become angelic, but to become Christ-like. We shouldn't have a picture of sweet, chubby angels on a poster or note card as our reference point for godliness. What would such a picture tell us about character except that angels are supposedly smiley and relaxed-looking? We remember also that our goal is not to impress the neighbors or to have outwardly "better" children, but to please our heavenly Father.

As we set about the task of raising godly children (remembering that it is definitely a task we have been given, one for which we as parents will give an account) we would be wise to remember that we are God's children. He is not embarrassed by us, but delights in us. He knows from whence we came, and He knows where we are going. It is all joy to Him. He has promised to complete what He has begun in us. And He tells us in His Word that it should be all joy to us. Our children are neither demons nor angels. Neither are they, in the end, our children. We are but blessed stewards of these wonderful gifts from the Lord; they are His children just as we are. Let us then strive to keep them from stumbling, working for their sanctification, knowing that it is a gift from the Lord and He takes pleasure in our labors.

Chapter Four

Diligence

In the various roles we have been given by God, an important aspect in all of them is diligence. We want to be women after God's own heart, women who begin the race well and finish it well. Often this comes down to not only knowing God's Word, but being diligent and faithful to apply it. The habits in our lives and those of our children help to shape the little spheres in which we live. We would do well to thoughtfully consider how God would have us conduct ourselves, and by His divine aid, set about doing it.

Achan at the Checkout Line

As Christians, it is possible and sometimes good to plunder the Egyptians. That Achan took the accursed thing doesn't mean that we should never seek plunder. But it does mean that we should be wary of the accursed. The devil's goal is to confuse us on this issue, and to disguise the accursed as things that are permissible for plundering. Add to that our own sinful tendencies of rationalizing which things are acceptable and it can get pretty confusing sometimes what we should do.

I have spent a great deal of time in these pages arguing that women ought to be women and not try to be men. Part of what this means is that we are called to be keepers at home. So wouldn't it make sense to plunder the Egyptians in this area, to glean from them wisdom on cooking, decorating, women's issues? We all know, I presume, that those magazines for women that tell us what men really like are nothing more than eye candy and at their worst can be downright pornographic. I don't expect I need to make the case against reading *Cosmo* or other similar trash. But there is a "safer" version of the same thing out there that can also be a trap. We want to keep better homes, so why not *Better Homes and Gardens*? We want stronger families, so why not read *Family Circle*? How could the devil sneak in the accursed thing in a chicken recipe?

My husband has suggested that sometimes the mud is too stuck onto the pearls and that we therefore ought to leave the pearls alone. It is true that pagans can have beautiful homes, make delicious meals, and organize their storage spaces just right. But what do these pagan magazines come with, in addition to all these wonderful ideas? It certainly isn't a Christian worldview. But in teaching how to cook, decorate, and basically keep a home, aren't they at least being "conservative"? Yes, but that isn't the same thing as being biblical.

Some of the extras that come with those seemingly innocuous magazines and television programs are an encouragement of the "Martha mindset," acquisitiveness, and a fostering of idleness. The Martha mindset that I've confessed a tendency toward is confusing hospitality with an incessant need to perform in our homes. Sometimes this can be a performance with an audience of one (ourselves) where we lean toward perfectionism and having to have things "just so." I am mentally raising my hand in confession of this one.

When we take too much pride in handling the myriad details and chores in our homes, we can be seeking a standard for our own personal satisfaction, rather than doing all in serving our families as unto the Lord. For some women there is an internal push to compete with other women to be the "hostess with the mostest." I'm sure any of us that have perused those women's magazines can recall such statements as: "Wow your guests with this fine cuisine," or "Leave an impression that will linger." There is a thin line between wanting to beautify the home (good) and seeking the applause of other women or trying to beat them in this area (bad).

Women's magazines also foster acquisitiveness. Why don't I have this professional stove? Why don't I have these fancy antiques in my home? Why don't we have drapes made of silk or the newest hardware to tie them back? These thoughts are encouraged because incessant exposure to these magazines teaches us to think that that which wins decorating awards or monetary prizes for cooking is "normal." And don't we have a right to what is normal? It's not unreasonable to want to trade in my black fronted stove for one that is stainless steel, is it? My drapes are okay, I guess, (or I thought they were when we got them five years ago), but who wants to look at the same old thing day after day? Isn't variety the spice of life? I'm just trying to make things attractive for my family and guests. Madame Blueberry, anyone? Then of course, there are the ads. These are professionally designed to teach us to be less than satisfied. Ads and the whole concept of "Don't I deserve what's normal?" can easily encourage us to spend more than we should, and can therefore cause financial strain in our marriages.

Idleness can also, paradoxically, be encouraged. How so? Aren't those magazines encouraging us to try this paint technique, to plan our flower gardens with that arrangement or to shop for our Spring wardrobes in this fashion? Yes, but we enjoy the pretty, glossy pictures so much that we think, "Oh, I'll just flip through it one more time to get some more ideas," or, "I worked really hard today —I'll just sit down and relax with this magazine." So we either enjoy living in this fantasy world where there are no chipped plates and no beans and weanies or we get discouraged because we think we're not that talented or can't afford that kind of upholstery or don't have time to do ALL THAT. Either way, we are inactive and don't spend time where we should. We also forget to thank God for His many blessings and the things that He has provided that are way beyond what we deserve (namely, everything we have!).

If we are wise, we will understand that the devil is not just found in Hollywood movies, but he lives in that which is normal, conservative, middle-class. I'm not saying to never get a recipe from *Family Circle* or *Good Housekeeping*. But we need not only to be on guard against the temptations raised in these magazines, we also ought not to be overconfident in ourselves and our ability to avoid getting sucked into worldliness. We cannot think that being aware of temptations is the same thing as defeating them. I am saying, as we always say, that our assumptions must be checked against the Word of God. That's the kind of reading material in which our noses ought to be buried.

Those Daring Young Men in Their Dirty Dungarees

Everyone remembers the Living Room at home, despite many of us never getting to visit the sacred space. It was the immaculate room in your house that no one ever actually used. You know, with the plastic covers on the furniture, the lampshades that still had the wrappers on them, and that carefully placed area rug, because Spot left a spot. There is a connection, a ratio between an immaculate appearance and the absence of people in the room. The Bible says one sure way to have a clean barn is to not keep an ox in it. (Of course an empty stall will not plow the back forty.) In like manner, one way to keep a clean home is to never allow anyone in it. On a smaller scale, you can keep that immaculate Living Room by denying most folks entrance. The trouble is, if we're not in the house, then we're all out in the dirt. Unless, of course, we live in some concrete jungle. Worse still, some who do live in our homes actually prefer the dirt outside to the clean inside. We call them boys.

Recently our son Campbell, along with several of our girls and I, were listening to a storytelling tape we had gotten at the National Storytelling Festival. We bought a tape of stories called "Grandma's Boy." In one story the main character, Jack, gets absolutely filthy. You don't even want to know some of the things that were stuck to him. While we were listening to this story for the umpteenth time, Campbell said, "Mommy, Jack and I are a lot alike. We both like to get really dirty!" Now, what a thing to say! It was totally unprompted. We weren't talking about anything, just listening and laughing. Campbell's statement was heartfelt and most definitely true.

My grocery bills for bleach and other stain removers over the past seven years will attest to that.

All parents face temptations in child-rearing. Some are tempted toward being too harsh, some too lenient, some with being too rigidly structured or others too flying-by-the-seat-of-their-pants. And sometimes it's not just Dad who wants junior to be a mini-him. Too often, Mom wants a mini-her, and so tries to raise up a little Lord Fauntleroy. While we can certainly teach our sons to be considerate of our labors in keeping our inside garden clean, we must recognize that they are made for the jungle. Though they may still be young, their default inclination is out. They are, by nature, outward looking, and so have to go where the dirt is. That's why it seems to be magnetically attracted to their clothes, why they don't usually walk around the puddle but see how big a splash they can make right in the middle of it. We need to be careful not to squelch that while we teach them to honor our labors in our garden.

The first step, as always, is to have a grateful and humble heart. Let us remember that while we are called to tend our garden, the kingdom isn't all lily-white doilies and shiny linoleum. Let us also rejoice that God has given us boys and let us rejoice that they are warriors. We happily married our warriors and look forward to one day helping some godly young women to have the same joy in our sons. We should, in fact, be sending them out into the jungle. While this is easier for me than some of you because of the ratio of boys to girls God has sent me, we need to guard against the temptation of having our little boys help too much with our women's work. Of course your son can feed the baby her carrots or dust the baseboards, wash the dishes, or set the table. But be sure he is also out gathering kindling for the fire and tending to the livestock and that he spends a greater portion of his time doing that kind of work.

Let us likewise praise them in their labors, even if they got that adorable shirt we love dirty. Even if it was your absolute favorite shirt and it will take five washings before it comes out only somewhat clean, remember that even if you keep the boy in a bubble, the shirt will one day be no more. The boy, however, will one day be a man forever, unless we turn him into a girl. We should delight in the boyishness of our boys, praising God that He made them that way. Enjoy your son's collections of various outdoor stuff. Be interested when he shows you the dirt mound he made into a fort for his toy soldiers. Take delight in the clever way he builds a ramp for his bike or develops a pulley to haul things up into his favorite tree. In fact, be delighted he figured out that grease would make the pulley pull more smoothly. Granted, as women it is sometimes difficult for us to really see things from our boys' perspectives, but we should certainly not make them feel defective because they're not like us. They can be trained and expected, out of courtesy to Mom, to take their muddy shoes off before walking across the carpet, but they should not be expected to automatically think to do that on their own. Remember to encourage your husband to encourage the masculinity of your boy. Don't begrudge him the time it takes, nor the laundry it takes, for Dad to wrestle with his boy in the dirt.

Finally, remember that dirt isn't bad. God made it and He made man from it. It is both what we work and what we are. It is central to our lives. We should also remember as women that we need not be prisses or be afraid to sometimes get dirty ourselves, working and playing hard before the Lord and for His glory.

The Day of Small Fries

If you have been blessed with children, no matter how many and no matter how old, you probably feel like many of your days are taken up with "small things." That's not just referring to the size of your offspring, it's referring to the grandeur (or lack thereof) of most of the tasks you perform. I fully understand, in caring for our six children, that such work is difficult. When we had four children who were under five years old, RC used to tell me that we were approaching, if not already in, the hardest point in caring for young ones. He would explain that at some point, children become net gains in terms of their ability to help. Having nine children, if some of them are ten and older, is far easier than having four children six and younger. Our days are filled with meal preparation, clean-up, laundry, meal preparation, diapers, cleaning, meal preparation... and so on. It is easy to fall into bed exhausted each night, wistfully longing for the children to grow older.

This wishful thinking, while understandable, is actually folly. First, as Nancy Wilson rightly noted, being worn out at the end of the day, if you're doing the work God has given you to do, is a good thing. It is the world and not the Word that suggests we ought to not be tired. And we believe the world instead of the Word because we are, by nature, lazy. We think there's something wrong with the picture because life isn't supposed to be hard. Does Scripture say that?

Wishing the children would hurry up and grow up is also folly because it is failing to delight in the variety of blessings that God can send. All children at all ages are a blessing, but each are different kinds of blessings at different ages. For instance, while they may get more productive as they get older, they will almost certainly get less cuddly. And they're not likely to excitedly bring you a paper with scribbles all over it and say, "I made it for YOU, Mommy!" Third, this wishful thinking disdains God's calling in your life for now. No one particularly enjoys changing diapers, but neither do little children like wearing dirty diapers. We need to do this. We need to do it joyfully, recognizing that done in the right spirit, it is our service to Christ (well, it's our service to Him regardless). These mundane chores are precisely what we need at this season in life to sanctify us, otherwise God would not have given them to us. It is this garden we should be concerned with. If we are centered on our own sanctification, if we are consumed with tending our own gardens, we will trust that whatever our heavenly Father calls us to is necessary weed pulling. This is true even if it means we can't spend as much time in our literal gardens.

Even though our daughter Shannon's difficulties have often seemed unendurable (though mentally I understood that God would never put us in circumstances beyond that which we could bear), God has used her dependence to magnify for me the importance of carefully caring for all of our children. They all need us, special needs or not, and we should not despise the days of small things. With Shannon we see no end in sight to diapers; we see no time when she will become a net gain in terms of her ability to help. She has no chores other than, at almost six years old, putting her bottle in the refrigerator after we open it for her. She is dependent on us seemingly for everything, yet how much more we are dependent on the Lord. And how gracious He has been to use her sweet life to show us that. What joy she has given us; a boatload of physically hard work and financial expenses—but a daily reminder of God's care for all of our physical and spiritual needs, a daily reminder of our own inabilities in light of God's great power and grace.

Of course we must rejoice when our children do grow older, for that too is what God has sent us. We will miss them when they are gone from our homes, but should not wish it were otherwise, lest we less than joyfully embrace the circumstances God sends us at that time. For now, while we need to beware the view that sees little children as a burden or a weight to be shaken off at the earliest opportunity, we must also eschew the view that sees them merely as romantic toys. They are not objects to be dressed up cutely and paraded around for the fun of observing their antics. They are little souls that are to be nurtured and trained for God's glory and that involves lots of things that would not look at all romantic to the world (or to the worldliness in us).

In short, we must despise nothing that God sends our way, even that difficult hour between when our children leave the home and when they start giving us grandchildren. And if that delightful time seems too long in coming, find another young mother to "adopt" and help in her days of small things. We have several ladies in our church and larger community that have blessed me and others immeasurably in this way. It also helps to remember that this is not truly a day of small things, but a day of grand things, for we are tending our little sprouts, who will live forever.

The Glory in the Ordinary

Envy isn't shy about accepting our invitations. Instead it sits outside our door, just waiting to be let in. For too many of us, we are on a first name basis, sharing our coffee with it. Of all the silly envies we sometimes struggle with, one of the silliest is envying the settings of others. We read our favorite Jane Austen novel, and not only wish for our own Mr. Darcy, but wish we could have been born into the English gentry, circa 1790. Wouldn't it have been grand to sit about the piano trading bon mots between performances, all the while wondering if this one or that had a fancy for you? How much stranger is it that we sometimes treat characters and settings in the Bible that way? I know that I, to my shame, would often rather have been present at the Sermon on the Mount, than be grateful that I have all of God's revelation in the Bible. God gives me all that He has spoken, and I would rather have only some, and hear it live. In the same way, when we are surrounded by the ordinary, how easy it is to long for the adventure we find in the Bible. Most of us, to be sure, would rather have a sewing needle in our fingers than Jael's tent peg, but a little drama sure would liven things up, wouldn't it? We're not asking to lead the charge at the battle of Armageddon, but serving donuts at the USO isn't the most exciting calling.

It would be dishonest to deny that some times are more extraordinary than others. That every place and every age is important, doesn't mean all are equally important. But it would be ungrateful to miss how extraordinary the ordinary is, when you look at it properly. The same is true in the very nature of the heroines we find in the Bible. Besides Jael, we have Deborah bringing home a grand victory in battle. Esther was gifted not only with great beauty, but given proximity to power, for such a time as hers. With all three, disasters were averted in unusual ways. We remember their stories, and we remember their names. But then there are the heroines we find in Exodus.

These women of faith, though they are remembered, were not even named. From one perspective, they stood up to a bloodthirsty tyrant, and saved the lives of countless babies. They were Esther in their time, without the castle, jewels and robes. But from another perspective, they were humble midwives, just doing their jobs. That, of course, is where heroism is embraced—in doing your duty, quietly, wherever it is found.

Few of us, however, are midwives. Most of us are simply wives. Pharaoh has not ordered that the children we are called to bring into this world be put to death. No, this day, this place is different. Now Pharaoh does not order, but invites, indeed entices us not to destroy the bodies of our children but to sell him their very souls.

It is good and right and proper that we should see our calling in its ordinary light. We are not heroines of the faith, but are instead merely doing what we are called to do. One could hardly call it suffering for the kingdom, the time we get to spend with our children. Teaching our children how to read their Bibles, how to treat others with respect, how to sweep a floor and milk a goat isn't the stuff of grand adventure. All we are doing is preparing our children for eternity. All we are doing is rescuing them from eternal destruction.

Esther was told that to interrupt the king would bring judgment. The Hebrew midwives, no doubt, did not relish telling the Pharaoh that they were unable to carry out his instructions. But what gave them the courage to do these things was the long, uneventful pattern of prolonged obedience. What gave them the power to stand up to principalities and powers was the firm conviction that they were standing with the one true Power.

Of course there is a reason why part of us wants the adventure. We think we can only be sure of our own loyalties when we are shown them in stark contrast. If only, we seem to reason, I were put in the position of the martyr, where boldness leads to death and cowardice to life, then I would know that my faith is real. We would positively embrace death in such a circumstance, for we know there is life in us. The trouble is, martyrdom is the easy calling. Obey Pharaoh, kill the babies and live, or protect the little babies and die is the easy choice. It is the little compromises that truly tempt us, tire us, turn us. It is either the slow, slogging steps of obedience that cause us to grow in grace, or the slippery, small steps of compromise that cause our very vines to wither. It is only as we are faithful in the small things that He begins to show us that they were the big things all along.

We need to honor our mothers, those brave and heroic women who, in obedience to God and their husbands, blazed this trail before us. There was a time when training up our own children was in fact to risk the wrath of Pharaoh. Learn the names of these nameless ones, and thank them, not first for easing Pharaoh's burden, but for showing us the way. At the same time, however, we must never, because it is now safe, become blasé about what we are doing, what we have been charged with. We too are heroines, whose battlefield is the ordinary. May we, only by His grace and only for His glory, be found faithful. May we continue to rescue those whose future would be death. And may we, at the same time, live in peace and quietness with all men, as much as is possible.

Perpetual Laundry Machine

We keepers at home have many blessings in our work compared with our husbands. Generally speaking, unlike many of our husbands, we aren't dealing with cut-throat competition on the job. No one steps in and offers to change our baby's diapers for twenty percent less than us. No one sets up a rival house right next door. (Well, the government does, but who would be interested in buying their product? That's why they have to force us all to pay for it. No one would freely choose it.) There isn't a great deal of office politics to maneuver around. I've never found myself worried that Darby seems to be building her own little empire over in the lunch-fixing department. Erin Claire has yet to come to me complaining that Campbell left her out of the loop on the firewood project, just to make her look bad. Our commute to work is extremely short, though we do tend to have more than our share of chauffeuring duties. We are, under our husbands, our own boss in the day-to-day labors; everyone else in the house works for us. In my small business, I've already got seven employees! It's true I can't fire them, but who would want to? Better still, they can't quit. No one makes us attend seminars in diversity training to make sure we don't make others feel uncomfortable in our workplace. Nor are we required to write down in some procedures manual, step-by-step, every job and sub-job that we do so we can be easily replaced. There's another blessing we enjoy: When our boss hits on us, it's a positive thing. One homeschooling friend's husband, when he left for work each morning would instruct his children, "Tell your teacher I love her."

There are, on the other hand, certain disadvantages in our work compared with our husbands. Generally speaking, we don't get sick days. We get sick, we just don't get the "days." It is rare—though it ought to happen from time to time—for our boss to praise us at the staff meeting. There are some unpleasant tasks that most of our husbands aren't called to during their time at work. It is a rare husband indeed whose to-do list on a given day includes, "Wash the sheets where the three year old threw up this morning." (And blessed are we whose husbands help with such anyway!) What may be most difficult for us, however, besides the lack of sick days, bonuses and other perks, is the fact that a homemaker's job is never done. Not everybody is working for the weekend. Our work just keeps on going.

It is the very nature of the kind of work we do that it is repetitive. That is, while we are doing laundry, we are getting dirty the clothes we are wearing. Laundry is not something you "finish" (except maybe for the day) but is instead something you must always do. As soon as we have given our 17-month-old his breakfast, he seems to begin working on his appetite for lunch. We wash the lunch dishes so that we might use them for dinner, when they will get dirty all over again. So much of what we do is cleaning, and stuff starts getting dirty the moment we have finished cleaning it. How can we keep from growing discouraged in such circumstances?

We need to take a closer look at what it is we are cleaning. No, we won't be encouraged by looking too closely for spots or wrinkles. Even when we finish "cleaning" there is dirt we somehow missed. Most of us don't have to look very hard for those things anyway—they are all too apparent. Instead we will be encouraged when we look closely enough to realize that all our homemaking isn't simply about making a home, but is about remaking ourselves. We do the work for the sake of our own growth in grace. And we are in fact moving forward, making progress, getting cleaner. We are given a perpetual pile of laundry so that we can get the job done of doing our work joyfully before the Lord. As Elisabeth Elliot says, wash those dishes for the glory of God! Pray in thanksgiving for the family the Lord has given you as you clear the table or help your daughters do so.

We are given the task of not only training our children to work—to clean out the car, to fold the clothes, to change the baby—but to do these tasks joyfully, as unto the Lord. We have not finished our work in training them when they can get the clothes clean without setting in the stains, the shirts ironed without burning them. We are not finished with the work of training our children in these jobs until they are able to do these jobs joyfully, without grumbling and complaining. If we would seek to train them in this area, we must first have mastered it—or almost mastered it—ourselves. Yes, there will be days when we mess up. But overall, asking the Lord for much help, we should be growing in grace to the point where we accept our work cheerfully, delighting in it. Our children will learn from watching us, at least as much as they will from our verbal instruction.

Work, for husbands and wives, and for children, does not exist for the sake of rest, for the sake of the ending of the work. Instead it all exists for the end of work, our being made more like Jesus. Like everything else that God puts in our path, the pile of dirty laundry is there for His glory, and for our good. Funny, isn't it, that folding a bath towel would be a means of grace. Funny that cleaning the outside helps clean us on the inside. Funny that cleaning in time makes us clean for eternity. Funny that in losing our lives, we find them. Funny that I have to go now—there is laundry to be done!

Chapter Five

Protection & Peace

For those of us who have been given godly husbands, we have been doubly blessed. Not only does the God of the universe love us and protect us, our earthly husbands do as well. Cultivating a culture of peace in one's home is a high calling, but one with rich rewards. Knowing that we are pursuing tasks with eternal significance not only gives us peace, but the protection of our Lord. Being used as His instrument to create a home that is a safe and loving haven is a tremendous honor and gift.

Safe at Home

There is only one place of rest on the baseball diamond. Yes, you can stop and sort of rest at 1st, 2nd or 3rd, but it is a temporary stop; you are still in danger. Only at home are you truly safe. In this most logical, understandable and enjoyable of all team sports, that phrase "safe at home" is used to describe the ultimate goal of the game. For us as wives and mothers, it also describes the goal for our game.

There is a fundamental difference between biblical Christianity and feminism. Where are you safer—out in the world or in your own home? For married women, at home we are safe in the presence of our own man. We are under the care of a man who covenanted to love us sacrificially and who is the authority in the home. Thank the Lord that though it may be very rough at times because of our sinful natures (and no, I am not saying "because of our husbands' sinful natures," because regardless of how he fails, we are still called to submit) we have it much easier than if God had called us to submit to all men. Outside the home, we are in the presence of men and under the authority of men (particularly in jobs) who have made no such vow of sacrificial love—men who either want our labor or, delicately put, want us.

Staying at home we are actually safer from ourselves. We are free from the temptation of self-glorification, of seeking to be man-pleasers, because we are about the business of helping our husbands. Out in the world we are trying to establish our own separate (not covenantal) identity, trying to make our own place in the world. This is probably part of what Paul means when he says we are saved in childbirth. He is not talking about redemption through Christ, but the protection that comes through having children that gives us very real and important work to do. We are rescued from the temptation of feeling we have missed our calling. We know that our husbands and children need us and it is a holy work God has given us to do. As difficult as life can be with our mentally disabled daughter Shannon, I frequently thank God for her, partly because I know she keeps me from being distracted by things God would not smile upon. Her physical needs alone are very demanding and probably will be for the rest of my life. I have to walk closely with the Lord and keep my focus on what He would have me do—there simply isn't time for anything else!

At home, we are also safer from other women. I'm not talking about not having to worry about them hurting us, but about the safety of not being surrounded by competitors for our husband's attention and affection. We certainly need to pray for our husbands—that their thoughts and deeds would be pure—but God has not given us the task of going out into the world and defending them from other women. Out in the world we can easily be roped (really with no coercion) into a sense of competition with other women, either in terms of our work, or in terms of our beauty.

We are safer from God when we are at home. Of course we can never hide from Him, but we can escape His wrath by doing what He has commanded. Titus 2 clearly states that we are to be keepers at home; those outside the kingdom earn His wrath when they do not keep the home. Those inside the kingdom who neglect this duty invite His chastening hand. When we stay and exercise dominion where He has called us, we invite His blessing; we don't earn it or deserve it, but He is often gracious to give it.

Not only are we safer at home, but in some sense we ought also to labor to make our homes safe places for our husbands. Since his conquest and calling is outward, outside the home, we should make our homes like gardens, places of beauty and rest. This emphasizes our work as managers of our homes. We keep the home fires burning (getting the new vacuum cleaner fixed for the fourth time in a year) so that he has less labor to do on the home front. He has not been called to start the home fires and continually fan them. He certainly does have responsibilities in the home (i.e. "man's work" and raising godly children with our help) but if we are managing things well at home he has less labor there and more time for his outward calling or vocation. I know that I am abusing my husband's willingness to help me if my laziness or lack of a firm constitution keep him from doing the work God has called him to do.

Even more important in making the home safe for our husbands is what we call Rule #2: Peace in Our House. (We'll talk about Rule #1 in a minute.) We do not make our homes safe for our husbands when we constantly harp on them. We have to check that curse from the garden, where our desire will be for our husbands (meaning that we want to be in charge). Kindly asking our husbands about certain things we'd like to do or suggesting some things that need attention in the home or family, if done politely, meekly and infrequently is very different from the teaching in Proverbs warning about nagging women. Do you really want your husband to feel like he is safer living on the corner of your roof than beside his nagging wife?

The home is also a safer place for our children, if we are striving through the help of the Holy Spirit to be godly parents. No one should be more zealous for their godliness than we, so this is where they are most safe. So root, root, root for the home team; if they don't win it's a shame.

Growing Peace

The Bible, while giving husband and wife together the call to exercise dominion, gives husbands the outward call and women the inward call. One could argue that man is to make the jungle into a garden (Genesis 3) and the wife is to keep the garden a garden (also Genesis 3). His vision, while remembering that the most important tool for moving outward is the children, is nonetheless outward. Her vision is inward. It includes the pains of childbirth and the struggle against wanting to be the one in charge and ruling over her husband. That is our curse and what often causes the lack of peace in our homes.

No man, however, stays in the jungle all the time. No man can, for that is where the war is, and every man needs a rest from the battle. Our job as wives is to make sure our husbands can tell the difference between the war zone and the comfort zone. We often laugh about the proverb's assertion that it is better to live on the corner of a roof than with a nagging wife (Proverbs 21: 9). This warning, however, ought to sober us. And it's definitely not funny when you can imagine that that verse is speaking about you. And unfortunately, we probably have all thought that at times. Hopefully, with hard work and the aid of the Holy Spirit, those times become less severe (less of that drippy faucet too) and less often. When I have had a particularly bad day (and no, I don't mean because particularly "bad" things have happened to me, but that I have handled whatever has happened particularly badly) it is a horrifying thought to think of hearing a tape recording of myself—or remembering that not only has my dear husband heard my dripping, but so has my heavenly Husband (only more so because He also knows my thoughts). It is humbling and reveals how much need I have for repentance and calling on the Lord for strength to do better.

Rule #2 in our house, which I have referred to before, is, "Peace in our house." Rule #1 is related—"Speak to my husband with respect." This relates to Peter's wisdom that a gentle and quiet spirit is where we find true beauty. Or, to find a modern analogy, this is what Doug Wilson talks about in *Reforming Marriage* when he asks what is the aroma in our homes. Is it a delicious, warm, enticing smell or... well, you can think of something really yucky for the opposite.

Too often we miss the mark on having peace and maintaining that pleasing aroma because we are aiming to please the wrong person. We get uptight and destroy the peace in our house because we're frazzled from staying up half the night cooking homemade frittatas to please our friends. Or we have over-committed to things outside the home (some of them very good, in and of themselves) neglecting our foremost task of caring for husband and children. For you single young ladies—helping out with whatever your father has determined to be your role in the family's ministry (probably often aiding your mother). A major warning flag to you should be if you have done this outside over-committing without really discussing it with your husband. We also err in thinking that our homes exist for our peace, rather than that we as women exist for working for the peace in our homes. That is a big distinction.

Of course, we have to have reasonable expectations. You are not serving peace in your home if you are stuck in a crying jag because you failed to keep the peace such that your crying baby woke up your husband. It really bothers me when I hear of women who insist that their husbands take a nighttime stint of caring for a newborn as if he should "take his turn." While it is perfectly understandable to occasionally need some help in getting a little extra sleep when you have a fussy newborn, it should not be expected that hubby has nighttime duty; he has, in most cases, daytime duty at a job and can't take a nap when the baby does! If a husband has mercy, seeing his wife's exhaustion, and offers to rock the baby for a while at night, that is one thing. But having him "driven" to it by a freaked-out wife is another. Husbands, the Bible tells us, are to remember our frames and that we are the weaker vessels. But we can't use that as an excuse to shrug our shoulders and say, "Well, I am the weaker vessel, what can I do?" You can gird up your strength and do what you're supposed to do. Stop feeling sorry for yourself and whining and obey God. And remember that His grace is sufficient to enable you to do the work He has given you for this day. Don't sin further by determining that you can just grit your teeth and get through it and collapse into bed at the end of the day. That's not how God intends for you to live.

In working toward peace in our homes, we need to daily remember what our husbands long for. More than fancy meals, fancy lingerie, fancy anything, they just want some peace. Has your husband ever had some happy news to come home and tell you about (or in my case, to walk upstairs at 5:00 to tell me about) and you totally burst his bubble with a sour attitude that you dumped on him as soon as he walked in the door? Would you want to be greeted by that when you came home? Avoid the shame and remorse you'll surely feel later—just don't do it! We need to remember that our gardens are to resemble the first garden, as we labor to repair the ruins of our first parents' fall. Let there be peace in our homes, and let it begin with us.

Lords of the Manor

We want our children to like us—we're not just satisfied with the obligatory love—we want them to think we're "cool." We want their approval and because they are sinners, they want to withhold that approval when we require them to obey. We cringe sometimes about enforcing certain rules simply because we're the authority. I used to think "because I said so" was a horrible, nonsensical utterance from a parent's lips (and not just when I was a child). Now I realize that, while I wouldn't want to use it in every instance, this is a perfectly legitimate thing for a parent to say to a child. Your authority as given by God is enough reason for any non-sinful thing you ask your offspring to do. It is sometimes appropriate to tell our children what factors went into a decision (partly to help teach them how to make decisions), but it is not something you want to set up as a debate.

We provide for our children's needs. We demonstrate our self-sacrificing love to them every day. This is a good thing, but also something about which we must be careful. Children don't generally learn the principle of being self-sacrificing by watching us do it, they learn instead that others are supposed to sacrifice for them. They learn to get, not give. This is something that can't be taught just by modeling it. If that's all you ever do, they learn to think, "Great! The world revolves around me and my comfort!" They need to be told and encouraged to act on the biblical principle that he who would be first must be last.

Because it is their natural inclination to sin, we attempt to hide our authority from our children. We try to be their buddy instead of their parent. We want them to see us as their peer, someone who is a best friend. We will often put ourselves through all sorts of contortions to avoid telling our children what to do—make it seem like his idea, use peer pressure, manipulate circumstances to make him decide the way we think is best. Why not just say, "No, you may not wear that outfit," or "No, you may not address adults by their first names," or "This is what we are having for dinner tonight"? While it is certainly true that we want to be close to our children, that we want to be intimately (yet appropriately) involved in their lives even when they are grown, the first thing that parents are to children is their authority. It is ironic that this authority that we often want to shirk for some imagined popularity is the very thing that draws our children close to us and makes them feel safe and loved and thus, much more likely to show us their affection. How many of us have seen our children go in a downward spiral of disobedience because we weren't taking our authority seriously and making ourselves discipline as we should? We know that he who spares the rod spoils the child. This literally means he hates the child (Proverbs 13:24). And how many times have we observed peace returning to our home and contentment returning to our child's countenance when we appropriately use our authority in calling them to obedience? We conveniently forget or ignore God's promise in Ephesians 6:1 that obedient children will have things go well for them. One of the things that will go well for them is having a close relationship with their parents—and that doesn't mean looking at their parents as their equal, as their buddy. You can have a great time with your children and delight in God's giving them to you—but you are still their authority.

Another way we shirk our authority—especially when our children are young—is by giving them too many choices. Teaching them how to make wise choices is important but is a much more gradual process than many parents seem to believe. We give them too many choices too soon. Young children are not the best judges of what they should eat or when they should go to bed—so why do we frequently let them decide? We don't want to make waves or have a conflict; we want to be liked. They become wise in their own eyes, thinking they are the only authority they need. They don't need us and if it came right down to it, they don't need God.

God does not tell parents that they *ought* to have authority, but that they *do*. Acting as if you don't have authority doesn't change the fact that you've got it. To hide your God-given authority from your children or to use it in a way that is not honoring to God is to violate God's authority. This will look somewhat different depending on the ages of your children, but it should never look like anarchy. Teach your children, by obeying God's authority in this matter, that they are under your authority until they have homes of their own and that they will always be under God's authority—even when He takes them home.

All God's Children

In teaching our children and modeling for them what it means to be color blind, it is important to make the distinction in our parental minds between racism and curiosity. When we moved to Virginia and had a lot fewer racially different people immediately around us than we did in Orlando, I was actually concerned because I wanted our children to be comfortable and familiar with people whose skin was darker than theirs. They will notice those differences, and will also notice if our reactions are natural or uptight. If you blush when your child asks, "Why is Benjamin's hair so curly?," they will learn to treat secondary differences as primary. They will instead notice if the distinctions we make about people we see in the world are based on whether they are the seed of the serpent or the seed of the woman. That's a difference that matters. Whether a woman honors her husband or not ought to catch our children's attention far more than the color of her skin. We should all strive to value what God values, not only to pursue being set apart, but also to look for opportunities to let our lights shine. Our children will follow our pattern. Racism is caught, not taught, but is caught far more often than it ought to be. We think more soundly on these matters than we act.

Socialization is, both sadly and strangely, a common buzzword linked to homeschooling. Those who object to keeping their children at home will raise this objection more than any other. While homeschooling provides the needed socialization quite abundantly and thoroughly, we must be quick to point out that the kind of desirable socialization that happens with homeschooling should exclude any hint of racism. It's fine for our daughter Delaney to notice that her friend, born in India but raised in Virginia, has beautiful dark skin. We don't want to squelch her noticing the obvious. More importantly, we want to teach her to think biblically, in light of 1 Corinthians, where it tells us that all those in the body of Christ are differently gifted. We want to teach her that some are knees, some are ears, some are toes, but all are useful and necessary for building God's kingdom, and you can't tell which is which by their skin tone. We should desire that our children know that their brothers and sisters in Christ—though they may do things differently or have different strengths and weaknesses—are still their brothers and sisters in Christ. Pointing out that their eyes are shaped differently is irrelevant at worst, and a sign of God's delight in variety at best.

In teaching our children to value others' gifts and not dwell on things that are not essential issues, there are myriad ways this plays out. We don't reject child A because she doesn't follow our family's rule B—that you don't say "stupid." We recognize, and teach our children to do likewise, that different families do things differently. This doesn't make them outside the kingdom of God. We also teach them that this difference does not require us to change or "fix" family A. It seems as if this can be an especially difficult task for children from three to six years old. They tend to see things in much more black and white terms. More important than teaching our children not to apply our family's rules to others, we make sure not to reject other families who sing different songs or eat different foods. However, neither do we seek to be culture-less, with no habits and preferences that link us to our ethnic roots. We always ask our dinner guests and resident students about their ethnic background and their favorite ethnic food to cook. Sometimes it takes a while, particularly with younger students who are new to our home, to understand the question. They might look at us like we're out to lunch until we start prodding with more questions like, "What kind of meal do you ask your mother to fix for your birthday?" or "What was your favorite non-American food that you ever ate in a restaurant?" By learning these things about others, we learn more about who they are. Some cultural differences are moral (such as celebrating Kwanzaa or Hanukkah) and thus we are obligated to reject multiculturalism per se. We teach them to reject the things that our Lord would reject. We don't say, "Oh, that's nice, it's part of your culture, so that's O.K. for you to do." We teach our children not to strive to be hip in the eyes of the world by acting like moral ugliness is just a neutral issue. Some cultural differences, though, are just different colors on the canvas. We have to carefully teach our children to distinguish between these two options, being first diligent to do it ourselves. We have to teach them, as we must teach ourselves, to be deliberate.

The balance we always need to strike is helping our children to understand who they are as children of the King. Our battle is not with another skin color, or another ethnic heritage. Rather, our battle is with another worldview. When our children understand that they are Sprouls, they understand that what defines them is their relationship to Jesus. He is the One who makes us who we are, a set-apart, holy people. And now, twelve years after we arrived in Virginia, God has placed numerous children of different racial backgrounds in our home, in our church, and in our larger community. These, like the Sprouls, fear no man, and fear God. Seeing these wonderfully diverse children whose families do things differently than ours has been a reminder to me once again that I needn't have been concerned when we moved. As long as we are a part of God's economy, as long as our loyalty is to the kingdom of God, we will have what matters in common with those around us, and will have different tastes to delight us. We will be one with many, and with many we will be one.

Queens of Mean

We Christian women are especially vulnerable to the nice/weak bait and switch. We easily waffle, when confronted, into equating being firm with being mean. We feel strongly the temptation to be wimpy sometimes—we're more concerned with being popular than with doing the right thing. We want others to like us, which means we want to be nice, which means we are often weak when we should be strong. We tend to think of aggressive behavior as a masculine trait, and for good reason. The man's call is outward—taking dominion "out there," taming the jungle, while a woman's call is more inward—being fruitful and ministering in the home. But an inward call isn't the same thing as embracing passivity. It doesn't, or at least shouldn't, equate with weakness.

Watching feminists seek to obliterate the differences between men and women, we notice that they often do so by acting aggressive. It's not so surprising, is it? It makes sense that since they are undertaking an impossible task, they might think they'd be more successful if they put more "umph" into it. Or maybe they think that if they raise enough of a ruckus, the rest of us would be so distracted that we couldn't think straight and we would just agree in order to calm things down. Their tactics are ironically insulting to women as they don't give all of us credit for being able to think logically. But because feminists do so often act aggressive and domineering, we Christian women tend to flee the other way; we adopt the languishing Victorian woman as our model of femininity.

We, as conservative, antithesis-thinking women miss the boat here, or fall off the other side of the horse.

Our call is indeed inward, to guard as well as to beautify the garden while our husbands expand it. We are called, as Paul says, to be keepers at home. This isn't a call to passivity and weakness, to being "nice," but a call to aggressive care over our flock. To twist the metaphors a bit more, from garden to fowl to bears—we ought to be like mother bears are with their cubs. If someone is messing with her cubs, a mother bear isn't going to sweetly entreat that person to stop. She doesn't seek to appear non-threatening, but rather shows that she is indeed threatening. She's going to aggressively make sure that the threat to the cubs is dispatched, and in such a way that it won't want to return.

We need to protect the center of our garden: our children. This is an active role and one often overlooked. It is also one where we can extend that sphere beyond where we should, seeking to protect our husbands too. This is often done out of love, but is wrong nonetheless. We don't have authority over our men. This means we are not responsible for their protection either. They weren't meant to hide behind our skirts.

In the right exercise of protection of our children, there are several areas we need to focus on. We need to protect them first from themselves, from their own sinful inclinations. Haven't you seen a child out of control, wallowing in his sin, and he seems to be screaming, "Somebody please tell me 'NO!'"? Our children need us to rein them in, to put a stop to their sinning when they are unable to. This of course is done not only with our instruction and discipline, but with the Holy Spirit's aid.

Be careful not to confuse this protection of our children from their own sin with the desire we sometimes have to protect our sons from skinning their knees. Our friend Monique told me once, when her son had climbed so high in a tree that she could see him from their second story window, that she had to just not look. She didn't want to stunt his masculine growth by causing him to be timid.

We also need to protect our children from our own sinful inclinations by not allowing ourselves to blow up at them. "I've had it!" and "I can't take this anymore!" are things they need to be protected from hearing. We don't become bears *to* our cubs, but *for* our cubs. This means we need to pray for self-control and zip our lips! And we all know that the latter is not a nice, languishing activity; it takes major strength! We need to protect them also from the roving lions out there by bathing them in prayer. And we need to protect them from the world around them.

Protecting them from these various dangers will sometimes mean being the bear. We don't act "nice" when our next-door neighbor offers to take one of our children off to an inappropriate-movie-laced sleepover. We don't act "nice" to the salesman who comes around wanting to sign our daughter up for *Teen* magazine or our son for *Rolling Stone*. In short, I do not protect my reputation as a sweetheart of a person, as the Queen of Nice at the expense of the protection of my children. We have to be nice enough to be thought mean by those around us who do not and cannot understand the convictions we have. Remember that we are blessed when we are persecuted for righteousness' sake. Don't let the pagans get you down.

We are called to act on our convictions with firmness. We don't need to roar like a bear at the neighbors who are trying to get at our kids. All we need to do is stand between them and those who would seek to hurt them. All we need is a quiet strength from the Lord that is undeniable and will make others think twice before messing with our cubs.

Mr. Worldly Wise

One of the delights of homeschooling is the maintaining of innocence. Look into the eyes of just about any homeschooled child, whatever his age. Compare what you see there with what you would see looking into the eyes of someone not homeschooled. You know what I'm talking about—that purity and cleanness is undeniable. Of course we understand that we were all conceived in sin, including homeschooled kids. Not one of us stands innocent before the throne of God. Not one of us goes one single day without sinning myriad times in thought, word, and deed. When we talk about this innocence in the eyes we are not talking about ignorance; we are referring to a look of openness and trust. This trust is a deep trust in God and in one's parents as the ones leading them into wisdom. The cause of this trust would be hard to trace specifically, but a big part of it is a lack of exposure to the folly of the world, the refusal to allow our children to be seduced by Mr. Worldly Wise. This is why we are accused of sheltering our children. Don't forget the succinct way to reply: "Next you'll accuse me of feeding and clothing them too!"

We know that too often when children are age- segregated what results is pooled ignorance. They all seem to descend to the lowest common denominator. As Chuck Swindoll so ably said, "When a glove falls into the dirt, the dirt doesn't get all glovey!" We know also that it is often the most worldly in the group that will draw the biggest crowd. Even little children are titillated by the sins of their peers. Even the times they wouldn't think of committing a particular sin, they usually will enjoy watching someone else do it. We are all like this, in our sinful heart of hearts. And just as with Pilgrim, we often confuse worldliness with wisdom, ennui with sagacity.

We have also drunk from the well of worldliness in that we have adopted a moral egalitarianism. If I let my child play with this one, then all of my children have to be able to play with any of them. But the Bible tells parents to teach their children to choose their friends wisely in Proverbs 13:20. This means helping them learn how to distinguish which friends will encourage them to godliness and necessitates making distinctions. Yes, you may play with Suzy Q and her sisters because they obey their parents. No, you may not go to the skating party of the girl you met at the horse show who rolls her eyes and talks ugly to her mother. We must teach them to distinguish between the wise and foolish. You might, with the last scenario, give your child the picture of the "ravens of the valley plucking out" that rolling eyeball.

We start the process of shunning worldliness by not succumbing to age-segregation. Mommy and Daddy, while an authority and not the child's "buddy" are the source of the child's identity. That's part of why God puts us in families and doesn't put our daughter Erin Claire in a group of other two-year-olds to raise her. Can you imagine? The invitation to worldliness is an invitation away from the child's own self-consciousness. Isn't part of worldliness wanting to blend in and be like everyone else? Disobeying Mommy and Daddy, when you identify with them, is like disobeying yourself.

Next in the anti-worldliness crusade is not being shy in talking to our children. We first distinguish between the children of God and the children of the devil, not being too politically correct to refer to them that way. After all, that's how God's Word refers to them. They need to be told that there are non-Christian kids out there who can lead them astray. Until you know your children have control of their tongues, you might not want to name any names lest they inappropriately announce that information to one and all.

Here's the hard part (hope you didn't think we got to that already!): This needs to be done in the church as well. We warn our children, in humility, and in the context of our own repentance, "Be careful with pew-neighbor B; he has a tendency not to be gentle with girls." "Be careful with sister C, she likes to keep secrets and encourages others to do the same." It might be a general warning about these types of sins, or it might involve naming names. While doing this, we need to also remember our own weaknesses and particular sins, teaching that except for the grace of God we would be committing those sins and that we also sin daily. We can also warn them against self-righteousness and point out different bad things that others could learn from following us! All of this means grace toward and honesty with other parents. That is, we do not say, "My child cannot play with sinners," because we are all sinners. But it may mean, if I'm that concerned about the influence of this child, I need to not he afraid to say to my sister in Christ (or ask my husband if he thinks it would be appropriate for him to talk to her husband) that perhaps that child's weakness needs some attention. I need to also remember that another parent might at some point be coming to me with similar concerns and I should be gracious in welcoming this warning from a fellow believer. We all can have blinders on at times and faithful is the friend who helps us remove them.

Lastly, once again, steep them in the real deal so they can recognize the fake. No one who has biblical wisdom will easily fall for worldly wisdom. Especially helpful is their understanding of this wisdom: We are pilgrims on our way to the Celestial City, so don't live for the approval of men. How much heartache would we all be saved if we truly understood this and lived it? We must end where we start—the beginning of wisdom and the end of wisdom is to fear God. When we fear God, we fear nothing or no one else.

CHAPTER SIX

The Fruit of the Spirit

Being a keeper at home and tending your garden with all diligence, means pursuing godliness in yourself and in your children. When we are asking the Lord to bring about His will in our lives, we should expect to see the peaceable fruit of righteousness in ourselves and our children. It is definitely a journey and, to use another gardening analogy, it can be filled with rocks and thorns at times. Overall though, we should be setting ourselves to the task of seeking to be like Christ, showing forth the fruit of His Spirit.

From the Inside Out

As I write this, we are awaiting the birth of our sixth child (actually, our ninth; we have sadly lost three babies through miscarriage). As I think and pray about raising this child to love and serve the Lord, I wonder if He will be giving us another girl to add to our four. If He does bless us in this way, it makes me think of all the particular nurturing and training a girl would receive that is different from what a boy would receive (homemaking skills, child loving and tending, submission and learning to value what God wants to see in her character).

In an earlier section of this book, we talked about the cursed things at the grocery checkout lines, specifically women's magazines. One of the troubles with these magazines that we did not discuss was the problem of the covers. We don't even have to buy these magazines to be infected by them. Just looking at the "beautiful" women on the covers is a double whammy. First, it can destroy our peace by putting us under the same kind of pressures as all those articles on the perfect party or the perfect new decorating scheme. We may be tempted to think, "How can I look like that when God keeps blessing me with children?" Thus, we allow the stress of watching our diet, fixing our hair, purchasing and maintaining an attractive wardrobe, etc. to destroy the peace in our homes.

Secondly, perusing these magazines implants in our minds a false idea of what beauty is all about. Peter tells us in Scripture what our goals ought to be and he is far wiser than Helen Gurley Brown. In 1 Peter 3:1-6 we are given God's definition of what beauty truly is:"Do not let your adornment be merely outward—arranging the hair, wearing gold, or putting on fine apparel—rather let it be the hidden person of the heart, with the incorruptible beauty of a gentle and quiet spirit, which is very precious in the sight of God." Of course we know this passage, but do we really heed it? And do we teach it to our daughters? For that matter, do we teach this to our sons so that they will recognize true beauty when they see it and not pursue or accept a worldly counterfeit? We may be tempted to think our husbands do want the beauty the magazines espouse and that they're not so concerned with the inner beauty that can only radiate out from a woman who is gentle and quiet of spirit. Remember Isabelle the pig in that great song by Judy Rogers. She was all dressed up with a ring in her snout, buttons, bows and curls galore—but she couldn't be taken anywhere because her attitude was so ugly.

So how do we cultivate gentle and quiet spirits in ourselves and our daughters? We must first remember *who* we are and *whose* we are. We are wives and we are training up future wives (and no, I don't mean we automatically assume they will marry, but we do need to prepare them for that possible blessing). In this role, we don't need to think that WE make everything turn out okay. Instead, we need only to be faithful, to do our jobs, by God's grace, and to train our daughters to do the same. Nine times out of ten, not only are we grabbing for the pants when we do not exhibit a gentle and quiet spirit, but we have already grabbed the pants and have broken them in quite well, thank you, through repeated wearing. The irony is that they are not at all comfortable; part of Eve's curse in the Fall is that she would want to be in charge but that even when she mistakenly thought she was, she would be discontent.

How peaceful could you be if you were under the care of the most loving, most gentle, most powerful and most tender of all caregivers? If you belong to Jesus, that is exactly where you are. And the same is true for your children. His perfect love ought to cast out fear; this means we need to trust Him and not worry about the things we tend to get overwhelmed with—what curriculum shall we use, what will our son be when he grows up, and did I grow the right tomatoes? If we have no fear, then we can have a gentle and quiet spirit, a true thing of beauty. It's important to model (sincerely, of course) this attitude for our daughters. Exhorting them about this 1 Peter passage will be totally useless if they constantly see you flipping out about your work, or the ants in the kitchen cabinet or all the weeds you meant to pull but couldn't. Attempting to teach our daughters God's truth is a humbling prospect, especially on those days when we feel like we've failed in many ways. God, however, can even use a miserable sinner like me to raise godly seed for His glory and kingdom building.

So is this type of beauty what our husbands really want? More than fresh baked cookies, more than a cover-girl figure, more than a rapier wit? Yes and yes again, this is exactly what a husband wants. If you haven't already—ask him. Beware not to use this godly standard, however, to justify slovenliness in your appearance. We still need to seek to please our husbands in our outward appearance, but this should not be something we tack on top of our pitiful characters. Remember also that this beauty is not equated with weakness, but rather with strength. It is the strength to do what we are called to do, while resting in the Source of that strength. It is the strength that is driven by peace and not terror, by gentleness and not shrewish domineering. More important than seeking to please our husbands with this beauty, we need to seek to please our heavenly Husband.

Right Side In

One thing we've unfortunately learned from the Freudian revolution, and that we sometimes take too much to heart, is that the inside of a person is the real side. That is to say, we think our real selves are the internal, emotional part that only we can see (except for those times we have some sort of emotional outburst, where our "true" feelings are made known). When we adhere to this worldview, we are less concerned with what we do than with how we feel. And if we feel a need to change certain things about ourselves, we have to really dig deeply, fiddling around while sunk in the muck of ourselves. We look at our childhood, analyze our dreams, blame our parents for our potty-training in order to figure ourselves out or to give excuses for why we are the way we are.

While we ought to beware this kind of hogwash, we want to affirm that we are more than just the outside. After all, "As a man thinks in his heart, so is he." Our actions are reflections of how we think and what we feel. The inside isn't the only side. But on the other hand, no one wants to be a white-washed tomb, sparkly on the outside, while inside filled with dead men's bones. It is not pleasing to the Lord to be outwardly clean but inwardly dirty. Man looks at the outward appearance, but the Lord looks at the heart.

This concern we should have for looking at things the way God does should extend to how we look at our children and raise them for the Lord. But before we get to their insides, we have to look at our own. We all tend to be more interested in looking good than in being good. Perhaps we're not overly concerned with our physical attractiveness, but we worry about what our actions look like to others (and usually those outside our families). How sad that we don't take the same care with our families and with how the Lord sees what we are doing. Note, for instance, how much more panicked and bothered we are when our children disobey in front of other people. We are embarrassed, or we feel guilty because their misbehavior is often a reflection of our neglect of diligence. However, when we overreact to their disobedience because we are embarrassed, we teach them to be hypocrites, just like us. We are teaching them that their sin is most grievous to us because someone outside the family saw it.

What we really want is changed behavior *and* repentant hearts. Another way of saying this is that we want deeds of commission without deeds of omission. We want our children not only to stop sinning, but to actively pursue doing the right thing. A child who merely doesn't do the wrong thing outwardly may not be growing in grace inside. We want them not only not to shove each other, but to love each other and look out for one another. We want them to protect each other and not want anyone else to shove their siblings either. This is part of what it means to have a covenant mindset. If Campbell sees someone picking on Delaney, he should see if there's something he can do to stop it (and if all else fails, yes, he may come tell Mom and Dad).

A good way to start working on our children's insides (or to continue along that path) is to encourage deeds of commission. Too often we see discipline in strictly negative terms—"Don't do that!" or "Stop that this instant!" We are also disciplining and discipling them when we say, "Yes, do this!" or "Focus on doing that more often. I like how you cleaned up the living room without me asking you to, just knowing it needed to be done." Or we can point out good heart attitudes when we see evidence of them, like, "It was sweet of you to offer to take Shannon outside for a walk." Encourage them in their growth in grace by telling them what the right thing looks like and most definitely praising it when you see it. Even if they're not as far along in certain areas of their character as we would like them to be, encouraging them when they're moving in the right direction is a big help. We are "spurring them on to righteousness and good deeds." While we are encouraging these good deeds, however, we must warn them against being white-washed tombs. For all our covenantal confidence, let us not fall into presumption. That is, we must call our children, as we call ourselves, to repent from the heart.

An outward, dead giveaway about our children's lack of repentance toward each other is if they just mumble, "Sorry," without even looking at their offended brother. You easily know that they are not truly sorry and asking for forgiveness. Another clear indicator of a lack of heart-felt contrition is if you hear them saying, "SHHH... sorry! Please be quiet! I'm going to get in big trouble!" In that case, they're more concerned about the physical consequences of their sin than the fact that they have sinned.

Of course, we must also be aware of our limitations. Don't become a Puritan, browbeating the children until they sufficiently manifest their internal sorrow. I don't need to say, "Darby, I know you said you're sorry, but I just don't see true remorse that you carelessly dropped that letter on your way back from the mailbox." Do be a Puritan, however, and pray with vigor and passion that the children will each grow in grace. Make this, in fact, a part of the liturgy of your life. Pray daily that God would be pleased to sanctify your children. And while you're praying, pray in repentance for your own failures, that your children will not suffer because you fail so miserably. Thank God also for your own growth in grace that your failures continue to decrease, a wonderful work of the Holy Spirit. In short, our calling here, as with everything else, as we call our children to repent and believe, is to repent and believe.

The House of Mourning

Many of us, if we homeschool, have been accused of "sheltering" our children. It's a strange thing to be accused of what you think wisdom demands. It's like having someone approach you incredulously and ask, with all due horror, "Did I just see you helping that little old lady across the street?" We do shelter our children, and rightly so. We would be failing in our duties as Christian parents if we let our children be exposed to anything and everything. Though the charge of sheltering has precious little to do with homeschooling, it is possible to shelter too much. Too much of a good thing can be a bad thing indeed. If our "shelters" are off-balance, run-off will ruin the foundations. Our prayer for our children is that they be innocent but not ignorant. We don't want their world to come crashing down when they find out that Grandma isn't on a long vacation and won't be coming back.

This sheltering thing, in short, requires something you can never have too much of, wisdom. We don't need to give our children all the gory details about certain things. You don't take a three year old through the Holocaust museum, nor do you explain the details of exactly how Simeon and Levi welcomed Shechem and his family into the clan. But if there is one thing they should know about from a young age, it is death. Some have argued that life on the farm helps with this because death is an ordinary part of life there. We first ought to let our children know, as much as they can understand, what death is. This explanation can actually go easier in the context of animals—either pets or the animals we eat. However, we should certainly make the distinction that animal death and human death are two different things. Children should be made to understand that the world to come is as real, if not more so, than the world in which they dwell. People do go away, to two different places, and they won't be coming back. We should not deceive them about these realities. This is likewise why we do not wait to tell our children of those blessings growing in me, until some arbitrary "safe" time has come. Together we have mourned for those we have miscarried, just as together we have rejoiced in the blessings He has been pleased to spare.

The most important reason they should know the truth about death is so that they can know about the death of Christ. And none of this namby-pamby "separation from God" stuff either. Our children need to understand that the Father was very much present at Calvary, actively pouring out His wrath on the Son. Our goal in teaching them these things is that they might know Christ better, and praise Him all the more. This is why we pray after discipline, thanking God that it is possible for Erin Claire to be forgiven because of Jesus' death on the Cross on her behalf. She can't understand that if she has no idea what death is. Again, this doesn't need to mean gory details. The Bible tells us plainly, even discreetly, about the death of Christ. But we can't miss it when reading the Scriptures. Death is spoken of in straightforward terms. Try to show them the Bible with the death taken out, and you have taken out the very reason they need to know the Bible, not to mention the Bible itself.

It is not just "death" in isolation that our children should be taught. Even in their youth they should be encouraged to think through the issues related to death. Why should we hate death? Because death is the fruit of sin. Why should we love death? Because it takes us to Christ. (Remembering of course that the "us" of whom this is true are those who depend upon the work of Christ alone.) Without painting overly vivid pictures of the torments of Hell, we must not teach our children some strange doctrine of justification if someone we love dies as an unbeliever. If God, for His glory, hasn't drawn someone we love to Him, we do not then hide that from our children. How should we mourn? As those who have hope. This too they must see in us—both the mourning, and the hope that is in us.

Here is one more reason—as if we needed one—to turn off the television. Our children don't need a cartoon view of death. They don't need to think that you can run off a cliff and run right back on or that you can get your head smashed with a giant weight and come back for more. They also don't need to feed on violence day in and day out (and not because we're afraid it will make them go out and kill someone). They need to spend their time thinking on things that are "true, right and noble."

Our calling in teaching difficult and sometimes scary things to our children is the same as the calling for every aspect of our lives. We are to trust in the grace of God as we seek, day by day, to be faithful, even unto death.

Tending Your Tongue

There are probably two reasons why warnings against some sins are given more often in Scripture than others. First, it may have something to do with the power of a particular temptation. It is certainly a sin to, for instance, put scars all over your body. But God need only say that once in Scripture and that is enough. Not difficult to understand or resist doing, at least for most of us. (Of course, once is enough for any sin.) Conversely, God tells us often to beware the temptation to covet, because it seduces us so often. I'm sure I don't need to give examples here. The second reason some sins carry more warnings in Scripture may be the damage that comes from those particular sins. Adultery isn't simply a matter of hurting the feelings of the offended spouse (though surely there is nothing simple or light about that); it sprouts all manner of other evils. Therefore, God speaks about adultery often.

How often does God warn us against the sins of the tongue, especially us ladies, and especially referring to gossip? If we are to beat this sin, we must face the truth that we are given to it. Perhaps it would help if we understand why. Women tend to be more relational, which means in part that we are interested in how other people are relating to each other. If, for instance, Mr. and Mrs. Jones are late for a dinner date with us, and we learn that they had a flat tire on the way, I would wonder how frustrated each of them must have been, since I already knew that Mrs. Jones had a difficult day at home. My husband, on the other hand, might wonder about what kind of jack the Joneses have in their car, and where they might get the best deal on a new tire.

This relational bent that we ladies have may be exacerbated (read: elevated to the nth degree) by our calling to be keepers at home. That is, because we are still somewhat worldly, we feel that we are missing out on what is happening out in the world or in our friends' kitchens and on their porches, etc. What is happening, I hope, is that our children are being fed and directed in the ways of the Lord and that we are showing hospitality to family and God's people. One of my husband's frustrations is that when he comes home, tired and wanting rest, I can't wait to hear what's going on, "out there." Did you see so-and-so? What did they say? How is so-and-so feeling? Anything happening with their house?

The solution, as with much of our lives, is that we must learn to tend our own gardens. That doesn't mean we don't care for and pray for others and their needs. We just don't have our world revolving around "news." We don't need to be the first ones to share information with others, and justifying it as a "prayer request." Encouragement to pray is a good thing. Needing to be the one in the know that tells everyone else is not. And if that regularly describes us, I don't see how we would have the time to be doing the things we should.

I need to know—do I need to know this information? This applies whether I am interrogating my husband for information or talking over the backyard fence with coffee cup in hand. I need to know how to stop gossip as well as how not to start it. I hate the idea of embarrassing anyone, just as I hate the idea of being embarrassed. But might we not help each other beat this sin if we make it our habit to politely ask each other, "Do I need to know this?" "Is this my business or would it just be interesting to hear?" I'm not saying we can't pass along happy news. Part of the question ought to be, "Would I say this in this way if the person involved were actually in the room listening?"

We need to remember—in this age of exalting information— that we don't need information, we need sanctification. It's not going to help me have a gentle and quiet spirit to know that Melanie had her nails done yesterday or that Rachel's new car cost how much?!! Insignificant information is not going to help me help my children pursue godliness. Also, I don't know about you, but I believe that adage about losing brain cells with each pregnancy. I can't afford to fill my head with information that doesn't concern me. Anytime I'm tempted to listen to something I shouldn't, I remember what we tell our children when they're being nosy about their siblings' business: "It's not your concern." We've taught them this so well that when one asks why another one was disciplined, at least one of them will say to the questioner, "Not your concern." Period. End of story. I should strive to be that cut-and-dried about my own need to know. We need to hunger to grow in grace, not to grow in being in the know.

And as always, we need to remember that there is One who not only knows everything, but knows us as well. We need to rest in His sovereignty, knowing that He works all things for His good pleasure. He will tend those things that are not in our gardens, because everything is His garden. He may use our prayers as a means to certain ends, but He will do just fine without our meddling. The world won't collapse if we don't know certain things. We need to know that He loves us, that there is our peace, our security and our adventure. Stop looking "out there" for those things that only He can give. We need to learn and remember this over and over again until we know it in full. That's one of the most important things we should seek to know.

Thank You Lord

When reading Scripture, most of us never go far enough with the images God gives us. For instance, Proverbs 31 tells us what an excellent wife looks like. Because we are the bride of Christ, Proverbs 31 ought also to inform us what the church should look like. In the same way, it is no accident that God makes the parallel He does in Ephesians 5:22-24. This tells us we are to submit to our husbands as unto the Lord. We should think about this in everything we do and say. We should speak to them and treat them as we would Jesus. That, by the way is a good test for our tones of voice—would we speak to Jesus the way we speak to our husbands? I know that is a shameful thought for most of us at certain times.

While it is true that our husbands haven't died for our sins, we ought to look at what we owe them in light of what we owe Him. Our husbands haven't died for our sins, but they do sacrifice for us every day. Few of you have husbands who think only of themselves. Most of us have husbands who work hard to provide for us. Most of us have husbands who set aside their own desires to do what is necessary to be the heads of their homes. Our husbands take the less comfortable seat, do the nastiest jobs, confront our sins. In short, they do die for us every day.

Submission and obedience are just the beginning of what we owe our husbands. What we also owe them is our gratitude. You may have heard the saying regarding children that obedience that is not cheerful is disobedience. This applies to our attitude towards our husbands as well. They want joyful and grateful hearts from us. If my husband asks me to be ready to start our school year on Monday and I sigh and complain about all the other things I have to do, even if I get everything ready, have I really been submissive? If I slam the kitchen cupboards while putting away the groceries, muttering to my children about how expensive it is to feed them, do I have a joyful, grateful heart? I know that nothing makes my husband happier than to know that I am joyful and grateful for him. I expect that most husbands are the same. After all, he loves you! He wants your spirit to be happy. He is investing himself in you, which is both cause for your gratitude and cause for you to let him know you are grateful. In other words, if you're really grateful, you can't hide it under a bushel.

I was privileged recently to listen to a talk by Doug Phillips. The discussion was about blessing the husband's vision. The wise woman is one who seeks to do this. Mr. Phillips was lamenting that he has regularly spoken to women who aren't the least bit grateful for their husbands. Everything that is said to them about what they're required to do is met with an excuse for why they shouldn't have to—he's not where I am spiritually, he's not in favor of homeschooling, he doesn't want more children. Mr. Phillips wisely encouraged them to get behind their husbands—their obedience is not contingent upon their husbands' obedience. How much more should we, who have been given much in our faithful husbands, get behind them? They will fail; we all do—men, women and children alike. We who are redeemed have been rescued from wrath. And He who began a good work in us will be faithful to complete it. Do not let your husband's sins keep you from doing what you ought. He is—assuming he is redeemed—on the same road you are to glory. The Lord is sanctifying your husband just as He is you. Your husband's imperfection prior to glory is not an excuse to let you off the respect hook.

The difference between a grateful wife and an ungrateful one is more often than not the godliness of the wife and not the relative godliness of the husband. As always, the path to joy and gratitude is followed by remembering three questions. First, what are we due? We grumble and are ungrateful because we forget we are sinners under a death penalty. Apart from the grace of God, I would experience torture and burning in Hell forever. That is what I am entitled to without Jesus. In relation to our husbands, we should remember that we were created to be his helpmeet, not to "feel" like the center of his universe in a romantic sense. The second question we need to consider is what do we have? Here a little honesty does the trick. We tend toward ingratitude and frustration because we think of material goods or situations for our families that we would like to have or that we even covet. We think we are due a bigger home or nicer furnishings or a great vacation or a more attentive husband. The truth is that God has bestowed upon us exactly what He wants us to have. Our houses are where He wants us, our furniture and vacations are as He deems appropriate and the same is true of our husbands' attentiveness. The final question we must ask ourselves is what are we promised? We should express our joy and gratitude to our husbands because they are leading us to eternal paradise. We led him out of the garden in Eve and he, in Christ, is leading us back. He does this by working to sanctify us by washing us with the Word, by praying for us and by calling us to repent when he sees us in sin. Thank your husband, because he is your earthly lord. He is like Jesus to you and so you ought to be joyful and grateful, today and always.

Greener Grass

The Scripture seems to suggest that there are temptations which have a peculiar strength to women. As a group, we seem to struggle with certain sins. Likewise, men have their own peculiar struggles, and we in turn have particular strengths. Gossip, for instance, is certainly something anyone can do. But women have a greater struggle with this than do men. And it may well be that while all people struggle with covetousness, women seem to have a greater struggle with this sin too. Or it could just be that our coveting is more relational, while men tend to covet things like their neighbor's horsepower, or socket set. We are prone to being dissatisfied and to comparing our circumstances with those of others. Our husbands, on the other hand, think if the grass is greener on the other side, it just means they have less to mow on their own. Women tend to grouse about the blessings God gives to others. But if we looked at it in those terms, that God has blessed Janie with a new wheat grinder, we would probably be much less likely to complain and covet. It's much easier to complain when we think circumstances happen at random, than when we remember that God brings all things to pass.

We do not beat covetousness therefore with stoicism, but with gratitude; this is part of the key to beating this sin altogether. We can fight our temptation to sin by building up the opposite virtue. In this case, that would be remembering to be grateful. All those complaints, muttered out loud or in the quiet of our own hearts—my husband is not as solicitous as hers, my house isn't as attractive or big as hers, my children are not as outgoing and charming, I can't eat whatever I want and fit into tiny clothes… I'm sure you know as well as I do that the list goes on and on. In pondering these things, or better yet, refusing to ponder them, we remember that we have the pearl of great price. We have Jesus. And we know that as Christians we shouldn't want to do anything but give thanks for whatever circumstances the Lord has seen fit to place us. All of our circumstances are the Lord's grace to us. So we must give thanks. The fact that circumstances are sent directly and purposefully from God has brought me up short more times than I can recall. Knowing that the sick children's dirty diapers, the sheets being washed multiple times and the children being bathed is exactly what the Lord wanted me to do this morning kept me from grumbling. I try to remember it's what He wanted for me today. Did you have an afternoon of sewing planned and the dishwasher broke and drained water all over the floor? Did you think that with eight children you were going to need a bigger house and then the Lord gave you a smaller one? Did your husband have a "better" job almost definitely within his grasp and then it didn't come through? All these things, as difficult as they are, are what God has deemed best for you. Aren't you glad and relieved that He knows what's best and that we don't have to decide? Has our heavenly husband not proven Himself faithful through it all?

The serpent is always working against us in these circumstances. He wants us to want. He wants us to find that which is beyond our reach to be "good for food, pleasant to the eyes and desirable to make one wise." This is another reason we must guard our eyes to guard our hearts. Thumbing through catalogs can seem like a harmless diversion, but what happens when we decide we can't live without something? Something we didn't even know existed before we began this harmless diversion. What if it's out of our price range or would take money away from something that is actually needed? Watching home and garden programs on television may look positively honorable. After all, we're just looking for ways to be better keepers at home with this recipe or that painting technique. But what if seeing sundry showplaces (and most of them aren't very homey at all) puts us in a position of envy and dissatisfaction? My house doesn't look like that one, my meals don't turn out like Rachel Ray's. Filling our thoughts and our vision with stuff has a tendency to make us lament that we don't have it.

There is a kind of godly wanting and longing. As long as we're willing to ask the Lord to help us do it, it may be good to think, "I wish I were as joyful as so and so. I know the hard circumstances the Lord has given her and she's still cheerful!" or, "I wish I were as peaceful as so and so. Her life has been tumultuous for years, but she just never seems to be ruffled or unglued. I know she has prayed for strength from the Lord and I will do the same." If we are going to "covet" that which belongs to our neighbors, we would be wise to at least "covet" their virtues rather than their circumstances. And in this regard, it would be more accurate to not say "covet" but "aspire to" or "recognize" their virtues and godly strengths. Even here, however, we need to beware. We can want these virtues as long as we rejoice that the Lord has given them to our neighbors.

Do not, in short, long for changed circumstances, whatever you might compare your current situation to. Instead, long to be made more like Jesus. That is why, after all, He has placed us in the circumstances where He has. We have Him and we are being made like Him. What more could any woman want? Oh that? Perfect, heavenly circumstances? We'll have that too, soon enough.

The Spirit that Counts

We were driving home from my sister's house. We had feasted with her and her family. There was both ham and turkey, pumpkin and pecan pies. My husband and I, in accessing the feat concurred on two positive reviews—first, the food was very good. Second, we were delighted to have enjoyed just a delicate sufficiency. We both managed to avoid the extreme discomfort that comes with the typical extreme feeding frenzy of the day. We had, by the grace of God, just enough.

By most people's standards we have had something of a difficult year. On New Year's Eve I was diagnosed with breast cancer. The next day my husband lost his job. A few months later, Shannon's seizures grew markedly worse. Then there was/is the house situation. We are without a home, and may not have one until next year. Two surgeries, chemotherapy, and radiation therapy and the recoveries therein filled the days in between.

Through all this year, my husband kept giving me the same message—now is the time to believe what we have always believed. How's that for support and wisdom? In case you don't know what we have always believed, here it is: "My brethren, count it all joy when you fall into diverse temptations; knowing this, that the trying of your faith works patience. But let patience have her perfect work, that ye may be perfect and entire, wanting nothing" (James 1:2-4). So far I have been spared this particular hardship, something I've imagined happening from the moment I was diagnosed—some earnest Christian squinting her eyes, patting my hands and asking with all sincerity, "Denise, what do you think God is wanting you to learn in all this?" As if our suffering prompts God to whisper in our ears what He's doing. We don't have to learn something new in all this—we have to learn something old, that God wants me to be perfect and entire, wanting nothing.

Our confidence in the sovereignty of God never goes deep enough. In the face of hardship we take some small measure of comfort knowing this didn't happen by accident. It is because my own understanding is shallow that I find myself behaving as if I don't believe at all. I grumble, I complain, I worry, I wish things were different. I do everything but count it all joy. Like a petulant child I look at what my heavenly Father has put under the tree for me, and I am ungrateful.

That's the root of the problem, what I want to find under my tree. It is because I am not sufficiently sanctified that I tear open boxes looking for comfort, ease and honor. Instead, like boxes full of sensible socks, I find fruit—love, joy, peace, patience, kindness, goodness, faithfulness, gentleness and self-control. To put it another way, it is because I am not sufficiently sanctified that my heart's desire is not set on what it should be, sanctification.

Even here, however, I fear I am not communicating it right. When we connect our suffering with our sanctification, it almost always seems to come across like some dire warning. We still think like Job's friends. The point isn't, "You'd better get serious about your sanctification, or else God will send you a stocking full of coal." It's not like He wants to give us gumdrops and Game Cubes, but won't because He's a wise Father who knows what's best for us. What I'm trying to get at is that God has carefully wrapped each of these challenges for me. He has picked them out on purpose, by design. He is unwavering in His commitment to make me like His Son, even when that's not where I want to go. But He doesn't try to make me like His Son so He can love me, but rather because He loves me He labors to make me like His Son.

Which brings us back to Christmas. Have you ever noticed our own peculiar prayer liturgies? Whenever people whom we love that are outside the kingdom suffer gravely we always pray two things—Lord, please relieve their suffering, and please use this time of hardship to draw them to You. Why is it that we only pray this for the lost? Are we so close to Him that we do not need to draw near? The presence of suffering in our lives is the assurance of His presence. Though we walk through the valley of the shadow of death, He is with us. And because He is our shepherd, we shall not want.

This is what we know. God is good. In Christ He loves us with an everlasting love. He has promised not only to forgive us, but to wash us, to remove from us every blot and blemish. He will wash us with His Word, and He will refine us with fire. He has begun a good work in us, and will be faithful to carry it through to the end, even when we wish He would stop.

I don't know what next year holds. It may be a bed of roses, or it may be a thicket of thorns. But I do know who will hold me next year. I know that He will not only hold me, He will mold me. Whatever He sends He will send with the express purpose of getting me to believe more and more what I am here affirming. I know likewise that whatever He puts on my plate, or under my tree, it will be just right, and cause for great thanksgiving. And so in the end we want nothing.